Helping the
Fearful Child

Helping the Fearful Child

Coping with nightmares and insomnia, school avoidance, toilet problems, and other childhood anxieties

Dr. Jonathan Kellerman

Contemporary Books, Inc.
Chicago

Library of Congress Cataloging in Publication Data

Kellerman, Jonathan, Ph.D.
   Helping the fearful child.

   Bibliography: p.
   Includes index.
   1. Fear in children.   2. Emotional problems of children.
3. Parent and child.   I. Title.
BF723.F4K44   1981   155.4′12   82-45415
ISBN 0-393-01392-8
ISBN 0-8092-5640-1 (pbk.)

Designed by Andrew Roberts

Published by Contemporary Books, Inc.
180 North Michigan Avenue, Chicago, Illinois 60601
Manufactured in the United States of America
Library of Congress Catalog Card Number: 82-45415
International Standard Book Number: 0-8092-5640-1

Published simultaneously in Canada by
Beaverbooks, Ltd.
150 Lesmill Road
Don Mills, Ontario M3B 2T5
Canada

This edition published
by arrangement with W. W. Norton & Company, Inc.

To Faye
and Jesse

CONTENTS

INTRODUCTION

Few things affects us more deeply than a child's suffering. We are bonded to our children, and their anguish becomes ours. The fearful child is particularly helpless and he has a unique ability to make us feel helpless. Parents of a child with an anxiety-related problem may initially blame themselves, even though such guilt is rarely justified. They may grow increasingly frustrated with the child for being unable to cope with fears. And if anxiety leads to the avoidance of previously enjoyed activities, parents worry that longstanding emotional difficulties will result.

Fortunately, many childhood anxiety disorders are relatively easy to pinpoint and treat. In contrast with learning disabilities, where causes and treatments remain uncertain, the origins of numerous childhood fears are evident. Anxiety reactions in children are comparatively easy to describe, and the psychological pathways through which they are learned are relatively straightforward.

I considered writing this book after treating many children who suffered from problematic anxiety and fear both in my private office and at Childrens Hospital of Los Angeles. Over the years as a pediatric psychologist, I had become impressed with how quickly such difficulties resolved themselves if certain principles of human learning were applied. Furthermore, my role in these cases seemed to be that of a guide—the children and their parents were the actual therapists. The key to success lay in understanding a few basic scientific facts, along with diligent application of this information. Seldom was it necessary for a youngster to undergo long-term psychotherapy for the anxiety disorder itself, and yet follow-up revealed long-term success. *Helping the Fearful Child* represents an attempt to record this knowledge for parents.

All children express anxiety from time to time. These reactions frequently are short-term and part of the normal process of growing up. In such cases, it is often advisable to do *nothing*. The distinction between "normal" and problematic anxiety is an important one, and is stressed throughout the book. Also noted are those problems which are of such magnitude that parents should seek professional help. An entire chapter is devoted to finding appropriate professional care.

I have made a strenuous attempt to avoid the ambiguity that characterizes many self-help books. My descriptions of general principles are often followed by specific examples of children I have worked with and exactly what I did that helped bring about positive change. The book also addresses itself to many of the questions that arise in the absence of any specific problem of the child's. For example:

How can I help my child to feel comfortable about medical and dental visits?

What is the most effective way of minimizing separation anxiety when a child attends school?

How can hospitalizations be managed so as to minimize the child's psychological trauma?

What is the most sensitive way to explain a death in the family to children?

What are the side-effects of watching frightening material on television, and what can be done once a child has been scared by TV?

Throughout the book I have referred to the child as "he," purely for simplicity, since constant use of "he or she" would be cumbersome. This in no way implies that only boys suffer from the problems discussed. When there are differences in the proportion of boys and girls evidencing certain types of problems, these are noted.

Though references are occasionally made to adolescents, the basic focus of the book is on the child from toddler through the pre-teen years. While it is not always accurate to use discrete cut-off points—such as child versus teen-ager—I feel that the problems of adolescents are sufficiently different from those of younger children to justify their coverage in a separate forum.

Two final notes of clarification are in order. The first is a semantic one. In the psychological and medical literature, a distinction is drawn between the terms *fear* and *anxiety*. The former is considered a specific reaction to a specific stimulus—that is, one is afraid of the water. The latter refers to a more diffuse set of responses—a person is considered to be generally anxious. I find this distinction more technical than useful when dealing with children and have abandoned it. The words fear and anxiety are used interchangeably throughout the book.

The second point is more substantive. The methods and

approaches described here are intended for use with an *otherwise psychologically healthy* child who develops a fearful or anxious reaction. It is unrealistic and even harmful to apply self-help techniques when youngsters are surrounded by *a continuing pattern of intensive stress.* This includes a child's exposure to divorce, marital separation, severe marital difficulties, prolonged parental absence, frequent family moves, neurological impairment, financial crisis, death of a parent or sibling, major physical or psychiatric disorder of a close family member, and alcoholism or drug abuse. The principles described in the book may work for such children if they are applied within the context of professional help. During major trauma or crisis, the total psychological milieu needs to be considered; it is often not the child who must change at all, but rather his family environment.

It is my hope that by increasing the reader's understanding of how fear is learned and unlearned, this book will help families—both parents and children—to enjoy the full range of rich and challenging experiences that life has to offer.

ACKNOWLEDGMENTS

I would like to thank the many scientists and practitioners—psychologists, pediatricians, and psychiatrists—whose research formed the scientific basis of this book. Specifically, those researchers and clinicians who refrain from imposing personal dogma upon reality and, instead, emphasize empirical observation and collection of data deserve recognition. Their efforts have helped generate an evolving, scholarly, and pragmatic science of child development and pediatric psychology.

My young patients and their families have taught me a great deal, and I have developed a profound respect for the resiliency of the human organism. It is a continuing pleasure and privilege to work with them.

My agent, Victor Chapin, of the John Schaffner Literary Agency, has been a steady source of encouragement. Special thanks are due to my editor, Carol Houck Smith. Her insight, rare combination of firmness of purpose and flexibility, as well as her enthusiastic support, were instrumental in nurturing the book from its inception.

Throughout my marriage, my wife, Faye, has remained steadfast, loving, and tolerant while I engaged in numerous professional and artistic endeavors—some fruitful, others quixotic. Her patience never wavered as I escaped into the stretches of solitude that make up the act of writing. Constantly I have sought and followed her advice because invariably I have found her to be correct.

My son, Jesse, has helped by being his delightful self. He has shown me that despite years of formal education and training, there is no substitute for parenthood when it comes to learning about children.

J. K.
February 1980

Helping the Fearful Child

1

Child Development and Normal Worries

Most of us understand that children are not miniature adults. Their bodies undergo rapid stages of growth and development and differ sufficiently from those of adults to require a branch of medicine devoted specifically to children's ailments. The same is true of the way children think. There are *qualitative* differences between the way that adults and children view the world and these become particularly important when we attempt to understand the origins of childhood fears.

The child's psychological growth proceeds from a state of randomness and generality through stages of increasing ability to differentiate himself from his parents, siblings, and all other people. Increased maturity brings with it the development of identity—of personhood. And as the child becomes more able to focus his thoughts upon the difference between what goes on inside his body and the external world, his fears and worries change, too.

For example, common worries of youngsters below the age of six tend to center around ambiguous and imaginary stimuli such as ghosts, goblins, and monsters. A four-year-old may not be able to understand that Frankenstein is not "real." In his mind, the distinction between reality and fantasy is blurred. For this reason, young children are said to be impressionable—easily influenced. Their minds are plastic and malleable, quick to leap at associations among objects, events, and thoughts that are not rooted in reality.

In one study, 74 percent of kindergartners described fears of ghosts and monsters while only 53 percent of second graders did so. By the time children reached sixth grade, such fears were almost completely absent—occurring in only 5 percent of the children. While fears of imaginary creatures decreased, other worries took their place. For example, over half of the children in both second- and sixth-grade groups talked about being afraid of injury to their bodies and physical danger. This is quite understandable because the older child has a developing sense of his body as something autonomous. Only 11 percent of kindergartners were concerned with such issues.

The especially rich fantasy life of the young child is also reflected in the tendency of youngsters below school age to report regular occurrences of frightening dreams. In the study noted above, *almost three-quarters* of kindergartners had frequent nightmares, while less than half of the sixth graders reported having bad dreams. Despite these differences, bad dreams are not unusual in any preadolescent age group.

The growing child also undergoes changes regarding his view of *causality*. Very young children are not able to differentiate between *symbols* and *actions*. When asked why they are afraid of ghosts, their answers are likely to be, "Cause they're 'bad' " or "Cause they're funny looking." In contrast, older children are able to distinguish a dangerous or harmful activity from a feared object or event: "I'm afraid of lions because *they want to eat me*" or "The bogey man will cut my ears off." After further development takes place— usually by the time the child is in the latter grades of elementary school—he will distinguish between stimuli that pose actual danger and those which he is unlikely to experience in the "real" world.

The following list summarizes the most common causes of anxiety in grade school children. Like any other developmental information, it cannot be applied with certainty to a particular child, because there are large individual differences among children. Nevertheless, such information will be useful as a general guideline for the parent.

NORMAL CHILDHOOD WORRIES

PRESCHOOL
Separation from mother or parents
Monsters, ghosts, imaginary creatures
Frightening dreams (often hard to remember or describe)
Animals (general)
Darkness, going to bed
Death (as abandonment or as personification of a monster)

EARLY GRADE SCHOOL
Bodily injury or change
Illness
Pain and suffering
Frightening dreams (easier to describe)
Animals (specific, due to some special characteristic)
Death (perceived as reversible, causing pain)

PREADOLESCENT

Injury

Illness

Physical danger

School performance

Physical appearance

Death (as it is understood in adult terms)

By the time the child reaches adolescence, the focus of much anxiety has shifted to an *interpersonal* context. Worries and fears are usually centered around the teen-ager's self-image. How he compares with his peers in terms of physical attractiveness, competence, and intelligence is a vital concern. Illness is seen as something that makes the adolescent look and feel bad rather than in terms of long-term effects. Since teenagers are heavily invested in achieving independence, events that infringe upon physical integrity and autonomy cause considerable anxiety. No longer is he afraid of the bogeyman or things that go bump in the night; the adolescent loses sleep over pimples, dandruff, mysterious lumps, and the shape of his body. Since he is beginning to think of the future, he is likely to worry about issues of career and education and what kind of adult he will be. This is not to say that the adolescent is consistent in his desire for autonomy. He may, while pleading eloquently for freedom, be terrified at the prospect of being left to fend for himself.

Some of the most common worries of adolescence are:

Looking different or ugly

Being incompetent—physically, academically, socially, or sexually

Being helpless or subject to another's control

Death—viewed in an adult sense

Verbal Versus Nonverbal
Expressions of Anxiety

We have seen how childhood fears progress from general to specific and from imaginary to realistic. One reason for this is the developing ability of the child to use *language*. Language is not only a reflection of the child's mental development but also a *cause* of intellectual growth. With greater language proficiency, the child finds it increasingly possible to think abstractly—in symbols. This, in turn, aids in the process of differentiating what is safe from what is dangerous.

The level of a child's language skills helps to determine how he *expresses* his anxiety. While older children are able to talk about what is bothering them, young ones often cannot verbalize their fears. Thus, while young children are the most likely to develop fantastic, diffuse fears, they are, ironically, the least able to articulate them. Parents who attempt to elicit such information from a young child can experience considerable frustration. The small child wants to communicate, but doesn't yet have the necessary verbal tools.

It is important to understand the value of *nonverbal* communication when helping the young child to express feelings of anxiety and fear. This includes the use of play, drawing and painting, as well as guided fantasies and imagery. In subsequent chapters, we will examine how such methods can be used to combat disruptive fear.

Sex Roles

Another aspect of child development that is relevant to our understanding of child anxiety has to do with *sex-roles*—differences in behavior exhibited by males and females.

Virtually every study of childhood fears indicates that girls are more fearful and anxious than boys. Other research, including some of my own, has shown that such differences begin to appear at an early age—before the child begins school. .

It in unclear whether the tendency for girls to be more fearful stems from an inborn difference between the sexes—or whether it is the result of learning. According to the latter theory, boys may be as fearful as girls but they are taught, early on, *not to admit to fear*. We can find some support for this notion if we examine the various ways in which children exhibit anxiety.

In cases where a straightforward fear reaction to a specific stimulus is present—such as a fear of heights or fear of animals—girls invariably outnumber boys. There are, however, more indirect ways that fear and anxiety can manifest themselves. These include stuttering, bedwetting, and soiling, and boys who have these problems outnumber girls. This may indicate that although boys are taught that it is unmanly or cowardly to express fear, their anxiety remains. It simply expresses itself in a different manner.

Common Symptoms of Anxiety

We would easily know a child is fearful or is experiencing elevated levels of anxiety if he could always tell us so. Unfortunately, such direct communication may not happen. The child may be embarrassed or ashamed to admit that he is afraid. Or he may be *unaware* of his anxiety. Such lack of awareness can occur at either end of the age spectrum, or anywhere in between. As we have noted, young children may not be aware of fear as a separate emotional state due to their lack of language labels. On the other hand, older children may find it so threatening to be afraid that they go to extreme lengths to *deny* anxiety. Anxiety may also express itself in ways that are not clearly related to fear.

The following are some of the most common manifestations of anxiety in children:

Changes in Activity Level and Concentration. The active child who suddenly becomes listless and unenthusiastic about things that used to interest him may be suffering from chronic worry or fear. Similarly, otherwise calm children may display sudden bursts of hyperactivity and shortened concentration when anxious. They may be unable to pay attention at school or do their homework.

Changes in Appetite. Loss of appetite or dramatic increases in binge eating are common symptoms of fear and anxiety both in children and adults. Anxiety may directly affect the gastrointestinal system, causing stomachaches and other discomfort. In addition, the energy spent worrying can sap the body's natural tendency to nourish itself.

Changes in Language Function. Refusing to talk for extended periods of time (elective mutism), *extreme* talkativeness, and stuttering are examples of the effects of anxiety upon the speech process.

Changes in Toilet Functions. Both bedwetting (enuresis) and soiling (encopresis) occurring in a child who has been adequately toilet trained have been connected to excessive levels of anxiety.

Changes in Sleep Patterns. Nightmares, night terrors, restless sleep, and insomnia can all result from persistent worries or fears.

Changes in Physical Movement. Anxiety causes reduction of physical coordination in some children. Movements may appear "jerky," "fidgety," or unrhythmic. There may be evidence of muscular rigidity, such as a tightened facial expression or stiffness of arms and legs leading to "old man's posture." Children who are tense often appear to be carrying the weight of the world upon their shoulders. They may engage in minor acts of self-destruction such as chewing or gnawing on fingernails or worrying a scab.

Obsessions and Compulsions. Some youngsters perform excessive ritualistic acts (compulsions) such as handwashing, checking various parts of their body repeatedly, prolonging everyday activities such as getting dressed or wiping their noses. These behaviors can be accompanied by recurrent thoughts (obsessions) that are hard to control. It is commonly accepted that obsessions and compulsions are evidence of elevated anxiety in children.

Anxiety Attacks. Sudden, inexplicable episodes of panic, during which the child clings to a parent and may have a fear of death or dying occur most frequently during the years before puberty and are most common in girls. Anxiety attacks may take place several times a day and are often accompanied by flushing or pallor, rapid breathing, dizziness, and nausea. Anxiety attacks may follow a fearful experience such as hospitalization or surgery.

School Phobia. Extended avoidance of school because of anxiety is one of the few overtly fearful symptoms that is displayed more often by boys than girls. The child may complain of nausea and actually vomit upon entering the schoolgrounds, or simply express feelings of panic and helplessness associated with attending classes.

Psychosomatic Complaints. Chronic headaches, stomachaches, dizziness, rashes, and fatigue for which no organic cause can be found can be due to anxiety. In addition, organic disorders such as asthma may intensify in the presence of elevated tension.

As we examine the range of anxious reactions that children can present, we can see how pervasive the effects of fear and tension can be. In addition, it becomes clear that many symptoms of anxiety are similar to those resulting from various types of physical disease. For this reason *it is essential that a comprehensive physical examination by a pediatrician precede attempts to deal with these symptoms on a psychological basis*. The child who wets his bed may have a minor urinary defect that can be corrected by surgery. The youngster who is fatigued and listless may be suffering from low blood sugar or a low-grade infection. Only after medical causes for a problem have been ruled out by a qualified physician—and for children this means a board-certified pediatrician—(see chapter 15) should the disorder be considered behavioral.

How Children Learn
to Be Afraid

The vast majority of childhood fears are learned.

This is an important and hopeful statement of fact, because what was once learned can also be un-learned.

Infancy has been described as "a buzzing mass of confusion"—from the infant's point of view. Babies come into this world with limited abilities to perceive what is going on around them and make sense of it. They do not experience themselves as separate entities and are not born with a strong sense of threat or danger. There are very few things that seem to frighten them. With the exception of sudden loud noises and sudden bright lights, both of which bring about a startle response, there are virtually no inborn human fears.

Babies are not afraid of heights. They remain relaxed while falling and have been known to tolerate severe drops without incurring injury. They are not afraid of snakes, sharks, or public speaking. They react placidly to wasps, mosquitoes, and bees. The sight of hideous monsters on TV often evokes only bemused curiosity.

And yet, as the human infant grows into a child, he picks up a complex assortment of fears and anxieties. How and why does this happen?

Fear: The First Line of Defense

Fear is a protective response. As the child develops a sense of identity, he sees himself as someone worth protecting, and he begins to respond emotionally to whatever seems threatening. Increasing awareness of his environment teaches him which objects are safe and which he must avoid. Some of this takes place as he experiences the consequences of his own behavior—few children place their hand on a hot stove *twice*—while other learning takes place as he observes the words and actions of others.

Don't talk to strangers, he may be warned. Look both ways before crossing the street. These and other messages are integrated into the child's view of the world. As opposed to when he was an infant whose welfare and safety depended totally upon the protection offered by others, the growing child is increasingly expected to look out for himself. The first step in this agenda of self-defense is learning to be afraid.

The protective value of fear and anxiety can best be understood by looking at the way these emotional responses affect the child's body. When a child is faced with something threatening, he may experience:

Increased pulse and respiration
Sweaty palms
Tense and rigid muscles
Rapid churning of the stomach and intestines ("butterflies
    in the stomach")

Feelings of cold in hands and feet (Caused by re-distribu-
tion of blood from the extremities to the center of the
body, this response is the basis for the popular description of fear as "getting cold feet.")

These changes are part of a purposeful sequence of events
triggered by chemical reactions within the nervous system.
This sequence represents an *activation,* or speeding up, of the
body resulting from a sudden burst of *protective energy.* The
fearful child can use this energy in confronting the fearful
stimulus (Fight) or running from it (Flight).

The *emotional component* of this burst of protection is
anxiety or fear. Thus, being afraid is a natural, normal, and
extremely valuable response. Without fear, the child could not
survive by himself for any length of time.

It is not only unwise but also impossible to attempt to
eliminate anxiety completely. Fear exists for a good reason
and the types of fears that children experience at different
stages of growth are often intimately connected with their particular psychological and physical needs.

One of the first expressions of anxiety in infants involves a
response to *separation*—being abandoned by the person to
whom they have grown most attached, usually the mother.
Separation fears assert themselves around the seventh month
of life, when the baby develops a strong sense of recognition
of his mother and is able to differentiate her from other people.
By expressing his distress through crying, grimacing, and fussing, he is attempting to protect himself against abandonment
and the loss of nourishment, warmth, and comfort.

The fact that there is a learned component to separation
anxiety becomes apparent when we discover that this response
is not uniform among babies. Rather, it is affected by the quality of mother-child attachment. If most of the baby's care is
undertaken by someone other than his mother, the loss of *that*

person will elicit anxiety and the mother's leave taking will be viewed with relative equanimity.

Fear as Life Disruption

If fear is a normal emotional response, when does it become a psychological problem?

In attempting to distinguish "normal" fear from fear that poses a true psychological problem, it is helpful to use the criterion of *life disruption*. Consider a given fear or anxiety response displayed by a child and ask the following questions:

How much does this behavior get in the way of the child's day-to-day routine? In what ways, if any, does it hinder his ability to lead a full, satisfying life?

Is the fear disruptive, in any *major* sense, to the everyday functioning of the *family?* This is important, because children do not live in a vacuum. They are members of families and the effects of their behavior upon those with whom they live must be considered.

For example, most children experience nightmares, and it is not unusual for bad dreams to occur three to six times a month. Knowing this, parents would do well to avoid making a fuss over such normal, transitory behavior. On the other hand, nightmares that persist, occurring every night, can disrupt the child's ability to function. In addition, such constant, chronic disturbances can be symptoms of a medical problem or psychological trauma. This means that the appropriate specialists should be consulted: first, the pediatrician, and then, if nothing organic is found and the nightmares persist, the child psychologist.

Let's consider the case of nine-year-old David, who is afraid to ride the giant roller coaster at the local amusement park. David is unlikely to experience much life disruption because of this particular fear and his parents should not be concerned. In time he may try to ride the roller coaster, if he is not pressured into it, or he may choose to go through life without experiencing this particular pleasure. In any event, his goals, aspirations, and achievements are unlikely to be affected.

David's classmate Lloyd is afraid of heights, but in a different manner. Stairs, ladders, elevators, and escalators all cause him to react with anxiety. Since these are objects which Lloyd is likely to confront for the rest of his life, and since his inability to deal with them will most certainly hamper him, he could be said to have a psychological problem. Even in Lloyd's case, however, fear is a problem only if it is *persistent*. It is quite normal for children to go through temporary periods of fearfulness. While it is impossible to state exactly what constitutes persistent behavior, the best advice is to use common sense. As we will see in the next chapter, most children have a marvelous capacity for handling their own anxieties, and it can be helpful to let this occur naturally.

Parents often question the *reality* of a child's fear. Many of the things that frighten children seem silly to adults. The Blob that ate Chicago may be nothing more than a few tons of strawberry jam, but to a child it's a monster and a menace.

Psychologists use the word *phobia* to describe fear that is unrealistic and out of proportion to actual danger. The person who is afraid of a smoldering stick of dynamite has good reason to be afraid, while the person who runs at the sight of a water pistol is phobic.

When dealing with the fears of children, however, the term phobia is not useful. We have seen that children, especially young ones, may not always understand the difference between fantasy and reality. To them the shark from *Jaws* may be as real as if they had encountered it in the family bathtub. If we really wish to help the fearful child, we will avoid labeling him as neurotic or maladjusted but will recognize that he is exhibiting one type of learned behavior. And no matter what causes an anxiety reaction, the child's anguish is very real.

Let us now examine how fearful responses are learned.

The Three Pathways of Learning

MODELING

Children learn emotional responses by imitating the reactions of others. This applies to joy and anger as well as to fear. The process of imitative learning is known as *modeling*.

The child is likely to model those people who are important to him. During the first years of life this means parents and other close family members. Later, the influence of peers and "admired strangers" such as movie stars increases. Even with this expanded repertoire of role models, the child will continue to imitate the emotional behavior of family members. The old saying "Do as I say, not as I do" is wishful thinking, for it is precisely what parents do that is likely to be imitated by their children.

The father who tells his son not to be afraid of the dentist but who himself turns pale seconds after entering the waiting room is transmitting a double message: *I say, don't be afraid, but there really is something to be afraid of.*

Action does, indeed, speak louder than words, and it should not be surprising to find that anxious and fearful parents are likely to have anxious and fearful children. This does not mean that fear is inherited, although there may be genetic tendencies for weakness that establish various parts of the body as targets for the effects of anxiety (resulting in ulcers, asthma, chronic back pain, etc.) I have seen adopted children who imitate, quite dramatically, the anxious behavior of their non-biological parents. It is clear that children do observe their parents for clues about how to react in the presence of danger. Modeling occurs in the absence of conscious thought or intention. A young girl does not deliberately imitate her mother's fear of dogs. Lacking much information about how to behave in the presence of dogs, she will imitate the maternal response.

Modeling is a very important form of learning because it is one of the main ways in which families transmit *values* to their children. Imitative learning is the single most important way that society's laws and norms are passed from generation to generation. Modeling contributes to consistency and is an important source of psychological stability. Needless to say, different societies pass down different fears. In America, rodents are generally feared. Parents view rats and other rodents with disgust and apprehension, and may clearly model these feelings to children. (Consider for a moment: Both the rat and the rabbit are rodents. An infant will not respond differently to them. Yet we teach our children, mostly through modeling, to react quite differently to them.) In some cultures, however, rats are eaten, and are viewed more with appetite than revulsion.

Many of the specific fears we model for our children are adaptive in that they help protect them from danger. Thus, it is no accident that turtles are seen as appealing while their potentially venomous cousins, snakes, are viewed with fear. In other instances, however, our rules about what is dangerous or repulsive and what is not are quite arbitrary. Why, for example, are ladybugs considered attractive while most other insects loathsome? Why are frogs amusing but toads revolting? Family A may teach love of dogs along with simultaneous hatred and fear of cats. Family B may model just the opposite.

The fears and anxieties of an individual child will depend upon the *emotional climate* of his environment. Certain parents set examples of adventurousness and reward adventurous behavior in their children. They encourage exploration and let the child know, often without words, that it is all right to take reasonable risks. In such families, skinned knees are not regarded as calamities but as part of everyday life. Such parents do not pressure their children to be tough or fearless, nor do they criticize shy or hesitant behavior. Rather, they set an example of activity and a willingness to try new things.

In other families, however, children consistently receive the message that the world is a terrifying place. In such cases the parents may have been fearful children themselves, never having mastered their own anxiety. They continue to exhibit fearfulness, so that family outings are accompanied by constant warnings to stay away from the water, not to go near animals, and in general, to be constantly watchful of danger. Children growing up in such families are likely to develop a generous repertoire of fearful behaviors.

At this point it is important to stress that parents are not universally responsible for every fear or anxiety their children exhibit. Today's child is bombarded with a much larger variety of messages from a greater number of sources than ever before. And traumatic fear can result from chance occurrences that are impossible to predict or control.

Our discussion about the influence of modeling in transmitting fear to children is not meant to bring about guilt and assign blame. Of course it is helpful to examine our own fears and to understand how they have influenced our children—if at all. But a more important reason for understanding the process of modeling is that this type of learning may be used to the child's advantage—as a way of helping him *combat* his fears and anxieties.

ASSOCIATION

Most of us are familiar with the Russian physiologist Ivan Pavlov and how he trained dogs to salivate at the sound of a bell by combining it with the presentation of raw meat. Pavlovian conditioning—*learning by association*—occurs most frequently in behaviors, such as salivation, that express themselves through bodily processes. Such behaviors, known in psychology as *respondents,* may be involuntary or reflexive in nature.

Emotional behaviors are respondents, too. They have a strong physical component and can occur rapidly or reflexively. Because of this, many emotional responses, including fear, are learned through association.

Children learn associations from the first day of birth, and possibly before. (The human fetus can be conditioned to respond to a musical tone while still in the womb.) The sight of the mother is associated with food and nurturance. Persons or objects that are associated with separating the infant from the source of nourishment quickly bring about distress.

Children learn to fear certain objects because they become associated, in some way, with threat or danger. An extreme example of this is the abused child. Abused children tend to be withdrawn, showing very low levels of behavior. Because of the high degree of punishment the abused child has experienced, he associates virtually *everything* in his environment with pain. Similarly, children—especially very young children—who are hospitalized and experience frequent medical procedures may learn to associate the sight of another person with unpleasantness and may shrink from being touched.

More common examples are the child who associates going to school with separation from his parents and who subsequently develops a fearful reaction toward school, or the youngster who is frightened by one cat scratch and associates his fearful feelings with other—or all—cats.

A child may be frightened by a movie and stay away from the theater in which he viewed the film. He may have an unpleasant experience with a bully with a particular name and wince every time he hears that name. He may eat a certain food while ill with the flu, suffer cramps and nausea, and forever avoid that food.

When an object, thought, or idea brings about feelings of fear, it is because it has become mentally associated with physical feelings of being threatened, in danger, or some other unpleasant emotional state.

It is theoretically possible to condition a child to become afraid of almost anything by pairing it enough times with something else that frightens him. An American psychologist named John Watson did just that in 1918.

Watson knew that one of the few inborn fears is that of sudden loud noises. By pairing loud noises with a white mouse, he was able to teach an eleven-month-old child to react fearfully at the sight of the animal. Basically, Watson did what Pavlov had done, except that his "dog" was a child, his "food" a noise, and his "bell" the white mouse.

Something else happened as a result of Watson's unethical experiment. Not only did the young child behave fearfully after being shown the white mouse, but also he appeared afraid of things that resembled the mouse, things that were white and fluffy. These included a rabbit, cotton, and a piece of a fur coat.

This tendency for associations to proliferate is called *generalization* and it explains why so many childhood fears get worse over time. The youngster who chokes on a piece of meat may at first avoid only meat. If however, his level of anxiety remains high, this avoidance can spread to other or all foods.

Generalization of fearful associations leads to increased life disruption. For this reason, it is useful to treat problematic fears as soon as possible, before they spread.

Fearful associations develop in the *mind of the child*, and are totally individual. They may occur between two objects, between an object and a thought, or even between two thoughts. For example, seven-year-old Joshua is swept under by a big wave during an outing to the beach. His fear may recur the next time he actually visits the beach, or it may be triggered by merely *thinking* about the beach. Children do not have to be exposed to something fearful in order to become anxious. Unpleasant memories can bring about the same results.

Erica is called upon to recite in class. When she doesn't know the answer, her teacher gives her a severe scolding. Erica experiences shame and anxiety, accompanied by physical sensations—blushing, palpitations, butterflies in the stomach. The next time she is called upon to recite, the memory of that first scolding brings back those feelings of anxiety. This may cause her to falter and hesitate, even though she knows the answer. High levels of anxiety have this ability to get in the way of the child's intellectual and motor performance. This is known as "blocking."

Here are some other examples of anxiety reactions learned through associations:

James has a difficult time with an arithmetic course. Every time he passes the classroom where his troubles took place, he begins to feel uneasy.

Susan is frightened by a penicillin injection. The next time she smells antiseptic solution, she is reminded of the doctor's office and her heart beats faster.

Monica comes down with a bad case of the measles after visiting a particular uncle. After that she refuses to have anything to do with him.

Often the association that triggers off the fearful reaction is coincidental. In Monica's case, her uncle had nothing to do with the fact that she contracted the measles. He was an innocent victim of his niece's mental association. Similarly, there is nothing inherently frightening about a classroom—it just happened to be the place where James struggled with math for an entire semester.

Such coincidental associations form the basis for what we call *superstitious* behavior, and adults are as prone to making these connections as children. Many actors, for example, will wear a certain piece of clothing on opening night and will become extremely upset if the treasured garment is missing. Such a ritual originates because it is associated in the actor's mind with a particular bit of good luck. Children are especially susceptible to superstitious behavior because of their fertile imaginations and sense of make-believe.

In summary, fearful responses can be learned because of their association, either in fact or fantasy, with something that the child perceives as threatening or dangerous. Such associations tend to generalize over time—they spread to new objects or thoughts—leading the child to become fearful of entire classes of stimuli.

Once again, however, it is vital to keep in mind that what has been learned, can be unlearned. Fearful associations can be broken.

PAYOFF

A third way that children learn has to do with the *consequences,* or payoff, of behavior. All of us behave purposefully. Most of our actions are not random. Rather, they are motivated and directed toward achieving various goals.

We do things that are likely to bring us pleasure. Such positive payoffs are known by a variety of labels: *Rewards, incentives, positive reinforcers.*

We avoid doing things that are likely to bring us pain or discomfort. That is, we avoid *punishment.*

The key to understanding the payoff principle is to appreciate how strongly behavior is affected by its consequences, by what *follows* it. Gary goes to school and does well. He may be motivated by any number of positive consequences—praise from his parents or teachers, the pleasure of doing well in competition with other children, an inherent interest in the subjects he is learning, or perhaps his father has promised him one dollar for every A he earns. On the other hand, his achievement may be the result of an attempt to avoid punishment in the form of ridicule from his classmates, or withdrawal of privileges by his parents. The manner in which consequences or incentives are set up in the family will have a major effect upon the child's behavior. It is interesting to note that when family norms and peer pressures reward academic achievement, performance will be at a high level. On the other hand, many dedicated teachers have reported the frustration of trying to stimulate children from environments where "being too smart" is punished.

The payoff principle operates most often with regard to voluntary behaviors. As such, it does not directly affect how fear is initially learned. It does come into play, however, in the *maintenance* of anxiety—in keeping fearful behaviors going.

Anything that the child sees as helping him avoid pain or punishment is likely to be learned quickly. Thus, after having experienced something frightening, it will be normal for the child to avoid what scared him. Though avoidance is a normal reaction, *prolonged* avoidance can be quite harmful because it prevents the child from gaining control over his fears and leads to withdrawal.

For example, five-year-old Connie has the misfortune to be stuck for more than half an hour in an elevator that is malfunctioning. During that time, her level of anxiety rises considerably, so that by the time the elevator doors open, Connie is straining to get out. The next time she sees an elevator, the memory of the traumatic event triggers an unpleasant association that causes her to feel anxious. In response to these feelings, Connie chooses to avoid the elevator and takes the stairs, pulling her mother behind her. This is rewarding, because it brings about a reduction in anxiety, and Connie is likely to repeat this pattern until it becomes a habit.

What is the problem here? After all, taking the stairs is

good exercise, and if avoiding the elevator makes Connie feel better, what's wrong with it?

First, elevators are objects that Connie is likely to come into contact with repeatedly, and there will be times when avoidance of them is unfeasible, or, at the least, extremely impractical.

More important, however, is the fact that *each time Connie avoids the elevator, she becomes more and more afraid of it.* Let us examine why this is so.

Suppose, rather than avoiding the elevator the second time around, Connie decides to take a chance and ride it. While she may begin the ride with a high level of anxiety, due to her previous bad association, by the end of the journey she may find herself saying, "Hmm, elevators aren't so bad." After several more uneventful rides she may find her fear diminishing until it disappears. And after still more safe experiences aboard the elevator, she may even begin to enjoy the ride. Through the process of *gradual exposure,* Connie will be able to master her fears by learning a new, pleasant association that replaces the old, fearful one.

Avoidance prevents this therapeutic experience from taking place. Connie tells herself, "Oh no, there's another elevator! I'd better tell my mom to take the stairs." The process of rethinking a fearful association leads to greater anxiety, so that something that once was only moderately frightening takes on terrifying proportions in the child's mind.

Fortunately, childhood fears are among the easiest to cure. While an adult may present twenty-five years of avoidance that have solidified into a habit, the child has had less opportunity to build up high levels of avoidance. Given a problematic fear, the benefits of early treatment are obvious.

There is a second type of learning by payoff that relates to childhood fear. Although being afraid may be initially unpleasant, *fear can bring about side benefits to children.* The child who is afraid of school may be allowed to stay home, watch television, and avoid the pressures of academic work. To the extent that this becomes a habitual pattern, he is being systematically rewarded for fearful behavior. Another youngster, afraid of the dark, is taken into his parents' bed while his brothers and sisters must sleep in their own rooms. A special privilege is offered as a consequence of fearful behavior—it is a reward for being afraid.

The benefit that results from problems is known as *secondary gain*. There are two common types of secondary gain resulting from childhood fears:

1. Parents may relax their standards of discipline or allow the child to avoid chores and responsibilities. While his siblings are still expected to assume responsibilities, the fearful child may not have to pitch in, because he is seen as fragile.

2. Attention. There is an old saying, "The squeaky wheel gets all the grease," and this is certainly true with regard to children and their problems. Parents frequently respond with extra attention to the needs of the fearful child. Though this arises from genuine concern and caring, it can lead to a shortchanging of siblings as well as to prolonging the problem behavior.

Attention from parents to children is like paying out a salary. Any behavior that consistently brings about a positive payoff will be quickly learned and may become a habit. Even negative attention such as scolding can be regarded by the child as rewarding, for it is preferable to being ignored. The child who consistently gets attention from his family for displaying poor table manners will learn that such actions make him the star of the show, and he will engage in sloppy behaviors habitually. The same goes for fearful behavior.

Most of us have observed the following sequence of events:

A young child falls and skins his knee. He shows an initial

reaction of surprise but no tears. Then, he catches his mother's eye and begins to cry. This occurs because behaviors such as crying are designed to bring about care and sympathy from parents. And, to a point, they are valid. By crying, the infant lets his parents know that he is in need of some sort of care, be it feeding, changing, or cuddling. Crying remains a stable part of the child's repertoire until it is gradually replaced by verbal expressions of need. It is likely to recur during periods of high stress and is a natural, healthy reaction. Of course, there are those children who cry at what seem like inappropriate times or exhibit tantrums at the slightest provocation. These are often youngsters for whom tantrums have been the most *efficient* way of bringing about attention and care.

It is obvious that parents should be available to offer comfort and support to their children during times of stress. However, attention should not be given *only* when children are fearful or helpless, while their masterful behaviors go overlooked. The child who grows up in a family where fear is the squeaky wheel that gets the grease is being selectively taught to be anxious and stands a good chance of being chronically fearful.

The word *chronic* is important, for it is the prolonging of a learned fear that is caused by positive payoff. In almost every case of chronic pediatric anxiety that I have seen, there has been some type of secondary gain that has caused the fearful behavior to last longer than necessary. In extreme cases, families have changed their entire way of life in order to accommodate the fears of one child. In reversing the process, a system must be established that rewards the child for gaining control over his fears and for successfully coping with his environment.

3

Unlearning Fear

In order to understand how anxiety affects children one must appreciate the importance of *control* and *mastery* as childhood goals.

As children grow (physically, intellectually, and emotionally) they are caught up in a constant search for mastery—for being increasingly in charge of their bodies and the world around them. In fact, the process of growth itself can be thought of as the systematic attainment of control.

A young infant's body movements seem random and aimless. Arms and legs flail about, and there is little ability to coordinate isolated motions into purposeful behavior. Gradually, these undirected, clumsy gestures give way to reaching, grasping, clutching, and bringing of objects to his mouth. The first, frustrated kicks of the newborn develop into smoothly coordinated "swimming," then crawling, and finally walking and running motions. In the area of speech as well, the baby achieves greater and greater control over the muscles of his throat and mouth and his rapidly developing brain begins to send messages that change babbling to more discrete sounds. These, in turn, are shaped into words, sentences, and soliloquies. By two to three years of age, most children are also able to exert some control over the muscles of their bladder and intestinal system so that toilet training becomes feasible.

As the child's ability to control his mind and body increases, so does his ambition. Whereas formerly he was content to bring his fingers to his mouth, now he wants to feed himself. The fourteen-month-old who was previously satisfied with crawling now wants to walk. As he grows, he wants to do more and more.

Anxiety as Loss of Control

Young children may have difficulty putting into words what it is about being afraid that makes them feel bad. Older youngsters and adults, however, are able to talk about being *out of control,* of feeling *helpless.*

Anxiety, as mentioned earlier, is a learned response. More specifically, it is *learned helplessness.* Anxious feelings affect the child so that previously learned patterns of control are reduced or disrupted.

Sometimes anxiety affects the child's sense of control in a physical manner. Examples of this are *bedwetting,* where control over the bladder is lost due to tension, and *fecal soiling,* where anxiety weakens control over the intestinal and anal sphincter muscles. In *stuttering,* anxious feelings about speaking can tighten up the muscles of the upper chest, throat, and mouth so that fluency is hampered.

Anxiety can bring about losses of control that are more subtle and indirect. The child feels helpless about his thoughts and feelings. Examples of this type of indirect loss of mastery are compulsive habits such as nailbiting and tics, which may start because they relieve momentary anxiety. As they persist, however, the child becomes increasingly upset about not being able to stop. Frightening thoughts that repeat themselves are also distressing because to the child they represent an inability to control his mind.

Losing control means taking a step backwards. We have all seen how negatively children react when they are accused of "acting like a baby" or "not acting your age," and how enthusiastic they are about imitating "grown up" behavior. Retreat along the road toward childhood independence is extremely humiliating.

For this reason, most problems involving helplessness are accompanied by a good deal of guilt and shame. Needless to say, those who chastise or criticize the child for not being able to control himself only make him feel more ashamed. Because shame and anxiety feed upon each other, this causes further reduction of control and makes the problem more severe.

Vicious Cycles

Chronic problems can be caused by the vicious cycles that are created as anxiety and shame repeatedly feed upon one another. Here's an example of how such a cycle gets going:

1. *Kevin soils his pants while playing ball.* This is normal for children of his age (seven years old) because they can literally *forget* to go the bathroom while concentrating upon a favorite activity. If no fuss is made, such isolated instances naturally disappear. In Kevin's case, however:

2. *His own sense of shame is increased* by a scolding from his mother (or teacher). A family discussion around the dinner table focuses upon Kevin's inability to control himself.

3. *Kevin associates feeling helpless and ashamed with going to the bathroom.* The next day, when he has to defecate,

his anxiety rises, and he loses control over his sphincter muscles.

4. *He soils again.* Another, more severe scolding follows. More guilt and shame. Less control. And so on. Kevin is quickly being conditioned to be helpless about going to the bathroom.

Most psychological problems of children do not represent unusual or bizarre behaviors. They are simply *normal behaviors that occur more often than usual.* All children have bad dreams, stutter, forget to go to the bathroom, and are afraid of monsters at one time or another. Excessive attention to these behaviors can, however, raise the child's level of anxiety, increase guilt and shame, and bring about a vicious cycle.

Big Deals Make for Big Problems

Families that make a big deal out of speaking clearly and rapidly are likely to produce children who stutter.

Families that make a big deal about eating, raise the risk of either obesity or anorexia nervosa (loss of appetite due to psychological reasons) in their children.

Families that make a big deal about constant success and perfection quite often produce offspring who become overly depressed and anxious the minute things don't go right.

We can prevent anxiety problems by taking a casual approach. We can also teach our children how to be in control, using the three pathways discussed in chapter 2—modeling, association, and payoff. This time we're using them in a positive way.

Therapeutic Modeling

In *therapeutic modeling,* we help our children to maintain a sense of mastery in the face of trauma or fearful events.

Therapeutic modeling lets the child know that we think he is competent, that we have confidence in his ability to handle things at his own pace, and that we expect him to succeed. Therapeutic modeling also allows the child to express his feelings and provides realistic information about events and objects that scare him. It involves transmitting the following messages:

It's Okay to Be Afraid. By letting children know that fear is a normal reaction and that everyone becomes afraid from time to time, we reduce feelings of guilt and shame. For parents who feel comfortable doing so, telling the child about one's own past experiences with fear can be very valuable.

Mom and Dad are people whom the child admires. They are seen as masterful and in charge. The fact that they have also been afraid helps to reassure him that being afraid does not mean weakness and is not embarrassing. Because they are no longer afraid of what scared them in the past, they communicate a positive message.

Being Afraid Doesn't Last Forever. Let the child know that fear is a temporary thing—the feelings of helplessness that seem so overwhelming will pass. This sets up an expectation of success and hopefulness.

It's Okay to Talk About Being Afraid. Expression of feelings is an important therapeutic process for children. By sharing how he feels about what scares him, the child is less likely to develop distorted or exaggerated ideas. In addition to conversation, nonverbal modes of expression, such as drawing and playing, are helpful. A parent can observe and listen, provide realistic information, and help the child distinguish things that are actually dangerous from those that are not.

It's Okay Not to Be Afraid. A parent who can be calm and reassuring when something has frightened his child is showing that it is, indeed, possible to respond in ways other than anxiety. When we model calm responses, we grant permission to children to be unafraid.

You Can Handle It, At Your Own Pace. Expressing confidence in our children's ability to master fears does not mean that we should pressure them to be strong and tough. Rather, it is important to emphasize their own, natural ability to move at their own speed in dealing with things that frighten them. Forcing the issue—such as coercing a child to re-enter a swimming pool immediately after swallowing water—merely serves to impose our will upon the child's. If we remember the importance of being in control, it is easy to understand how this serves only to make him more fearful.

Five-year-old Mary Ellen hears a story about witches and goblins from some friends at kindergarten. The other children talk about how these monsters can harm, maim, and damage children—how they eat them up and bake them into cookies. Mary Ellen, hanging around the edges of the discussion, constructs vivid pictures in her head. That night she thinks of witches and goblins and she finds it difficult to sleep. When she wakes in the morning, the fear is still with her. She approaches her father and tells him:

MARY ELLEN: I was scared about witches last night and I couldn't sleep.

FATHER: [agitated] Mary Ellen, I've told you to stay away from scary TV shows.

MARY ELLEN: But Dad, it wasn't on TV! The kids at school were talking about it and . . .

FATHER: I don't care where you heard it. Stay away from that kind of thing. You're too young for it.

What is being communicated to Mary Ellen in this brief dialogue? First, Dad's own agitated response lets her know that *he* is upset by the idea of witches. In fact, she may believe that her father is frightened by witches, that they *really are* something to be afraid of.

Second, there is a scolding, punishing tone to Dad's words. Though motivated by concern, his own feelings make him sound angry. In this way, he lets Mary Ellen know that by becoming afraid and talking to him about it, she has somehow misbehaved. Enter guilt and shame.

Finally, Mary Ellen's father's warning to stay away from things that are frightening communicates to her that she cannot control herself, that she *is not competent* to handle stress. Her father's words let her know that he does not trust her and that *he* will take charge. This is a virtual invitation to this little girl to become dependent, and helpless.

Now let's examine a more therapeutic approach:

MARY ELLEN: And I thought about the witches and I got real scared.

FATHER: [calm, drawing her close, physically] Witches? Oh yeah, I remember when I was about your age I heard a story about a wicked witch and it scared me too.

MARY ELLEN: Really?

FATHER: Sure. I guess all kids—and grownups—get scared once in a while. But it goes away. What scared you most about witches?

At this point, Mary Ellen may go into the details of the frightening story, or she may be reluctant to talk. Dad should not pressure her but should maintain a casual but caring approach. At some point, it will be useful for him to repeat something that emphasizes Mary Ellen's competence and ability to handle herself and to offer a positive expectation such as "Well, I'll bet the next time you hear about witches you won't have to be so afraid."

Notice that Dad does not attempt to shelter her or forbid

Mary Ellen from being exposed to what frightened her. He, in fact, assumes that Mary Ellen *will* hear about witches at some time in the future. And he lets her know that he has confidence in her ability to be *less* afraid (not *unafraid*) when she does.

Therapeutic modeling is not a cure for childhood anxiety. It is merely an important first step that sets the stage for open communication, parental support, and building the child's self-esteem. In some cases supportive reassurance will be sufficient in preventing long-term anxiety problems. In fact, many parents use therapeutic modeling without realizing they are doing so. It is a part of good child-rearing.

Even so, as parents we must accept the fact that we cannot always protect our children from unpleasantness, stress, and anxiety. When, despite our best supportive efforts, children become anxious for prolonged periods of time—in Mary Ellen's case this might mean her staying afraid for weeks, or showing other signs of anxiety such as restlessness, insomnia, bad dreams, or inability to concentrate—we should turn our attention to the second pathway of learning.

Therapeutic Association

The successful treatment of childhood anxiety always involves the *learning of a new association* to replace the old, fearful one. Children often learn such new associations by themselves. Parents or therapists may also help the process along.

Therapeutic associations involve learning behaviors that are incompatible with anxiety, that cannot exist in the same body at the same time with anxiety. Such behaviors are called counter-anxious responses, anxiety antagonists, or more simply, the *enemies of anxiety*. They are the good guys who help vanquish villainous fear.

Relaxation, a body state that is the physiological opposite

of anxiety, has been used to help adults and adolescents deal with problematic fear. The patient is taught deep relaxation through techniques such as yoga, progressive muscle relaxation, or hypnosis, and is aided in re-experiencing the feared stimulus while relaxed. Most children, however, find the passive state of deep relaxation quite boring and will not sit still long enough to learn it. For youngsters, there are more effective enemies of anxiety.

Imaginary scenes that capture a youngster's sense of fantasy are potent sources of anti-anxiety ammunition. The ability to fantasize is a talent that comes naturally for most children and it improves with practice. Children slip quite easily in and out of fantasy states. That is why they daydream, make up imaginary playmates, and show little regard for accuracy with regard to color ("green men with purple bananas"), size ("giant birds, two hundred feet tall"), or shape ("a house shaped like a lollipop").

Positive fantasies are often sufficiently pleasurable to drive away anxious feelings. For example, a child who is afraid of monsters may profit from imagining himself as a knight in armor slaying the fearful beast with masterful ease.

The therapeutic component of a counter-anxious image is its emotional content—how it makes the child feel. Fantasies that foster feelings of being in control are the ones that successfully fight fear.

Interestingly, many children find that they *cannot be angry and afraid at the same time.* This is because getting mad makes them feel in control. In such cases, anger is one of the most valuable enemies of anxiety that children have at their command.

Engaging in favorite activities, or imagining doing so, is another source of counter-anxious experience. Since favorite things vary from child to child, effective use of them depends upon knowing the child and being aware of his special preferences. Some common favorite things include going to amusement parks, playing games, spending time with a special person, or walking along a beach. When the behavior is at the child's immediate disposal,—for example, playing a favorite record the minute he feels afraid—it can be used in a straightforward manner. In other cases, the youngster can learn to imagine doing something pleasant.

For children who are not obese or do not have any other type of eating problem, *eating and drinking* are excellent anti-anxiety behaviors. This is because these activities are inherently pleasurable, perhaps most pleasurable to very young children who lack the verbal skills to communicate their fantasies. Infants characteristically fight fear by grabbing their bottle (or an oral substitute such as a thumb or pacifier) during times of stress. Children who experience anxiety at night can be helped by being allowed to get up for a snack. A young child who is afraid of a specific place can be gradually brought closer and closer while nibbling on some favorite food.

Counter-anxious imagery can be used as a technique in itself, or may be utilized in combination with other approaches such as anger and favorite activities. For example, if Mary Ellen appears to be suffering from prolonged fear of witches, her father might want to help her by encouraging her anger.

FATHER: Why don't we draw a picture of a witch, Mary Ellen?

MARY ELLEN [hesitant] I don't know how.

FATHER: Well, maybe we can do it together. (Starts out drawing a witch and gradually encourages Mary Ellen to take over the drawing. If she persists in not wanting to draw, Dad can finish the drawing himself.)

FATHER: There. [holding up drawing] Now what do you think of that?

MARY ELLEN: I——I don't know.

FATHER: Does this picture make you feel a little scared?

MARY ELLEN: Uh huh.

FATHER: That's okay. Let's see if we can make the fear go away. Do you know that you can't be mad and scared at the same time?

MARY ELLEN: No?

FATHER: That's right. Being mad gets rid of being scared, so why don't we start to get mad at this mean old witch and then we don't have to be afraid.

Some children will readily embrace the suggestion to get angry, others will be reluctant. If Mary Ellen hesitates, Dad can get the ball rolling.

FATHER: [stares at drawing] You mean old witch! I'm really mad at you for scaring Mary Ellen! And she's really mad at you too.

Most children will allow themselves to be drawn into a game-like atmosphere of getting angry. Parental participation offers the extra benefit of a shared experience with Dad or Mom. The use of drawings is particularly helpful in that they can be destroyed. I encourage children to attack drawings of things that scare them, then tear up the drawings and throw them away. This makes the child feel that he has overcome a dreaded opponent.

Mary Ellen's father will guide her in dispatching the drawing of the witch into the trash basket. If he senses that she is still afraid, he will repeat the "anger game" with another drawing, until she reports not feeling so scared.

FATHER: There, you see! We finished off that mean old witch and now we don't have to be so afraid of her. Do you know what you can do if you start to feel scared?

MARY ELLEN: Get real mad?

FATHER: That's right. Just get real mad and you'll see that it makes the scaredness go away. You can be the boss over a silly old witch any time!

MARY ELLEN: Can I do another drawing?

FATHER: Sure. Do as many as you want and just tear them up and throw out those old witches. And Mary Ellen——

MARY ELLEN: What, Daddy?

FATHER: I'm really proud of you and the way you can handle things.

This technique helps break the old association between witches and anxiety and substitutes in its place a new therapeutic association between witches and anger (being in control). Again, instead of sheltering Mary Ellen her father has done something much more valuable. He has shown her a way to cope, not only with witches but with other things that may frighten her in the future.

Therapeutic Payoff

As we have seen, anxiety problems can cause disruption in a family. Movies and television shows may be avoided because they might be "too scary for Billy." Overnight trips are canceled because "Elizabeth can't sleep peacefully anywhere but at home."

This type of attention gives the fearful child a good deal of power, but it is power of the wrong type. For he is learning that by being helpless, dependent, and fearful he can get other people to do his bidding. If reward for fearfulness continues, the youngster begins to think of himself as a Fearful Child, rather than as a child with a temporary problem. This can damage his sense of self-esteem.

Children *should* have power—they should be able to exert some degree of control over their environment. But such control should come about as a result of positive, not problematic, behavior.

There is an old saying: *A glass may be either half-empty or half-full*. It depends upon your point of view. We can choose between emphasizing negative or positive aspects of a situation. For every negative behavior, there is a positive counterpart. Even the most anxious child will exhibit some degree of assertiveness and control. It may be the calm masterful way he assembles a model. Or the manner in which he systematically attacks a problem and solves it.

The challenge for parents is to recognize such masterful behaviors and to reward them with praise and attention.

I have treated numerous children who suffer from chronic nightmares. In most of these cases, the nightmares do not occur every evening. There may be one or more days when the child sleeps peacefully. But family attention becomes focused upon the times when he does *not*. Parents may begin to allow the child who has experienced a bad dream to spend the night in their bed. This is a practice that should always be discouraged. Offering intimacy and warmth as the consequences of anxiety serves only to reward it. Meanwhile, on the days when the child sleeps peacefully, he is ignored. He is learning that it *pays off* to be afraid.

I regularly counsel parents to return to their normal living schedule and to reverse major modifications they may have made to fulfill the special needs of the fearful child. Children deserve sympathy and understanding. They do not benefit, however, from learning that the world magically changes because they have a problem.

It is not sufficient simply to remove the "rewards" that come from being afraid. We must substitute something in their place. Remember that the fearful child has learned a pattern which has become habitual. He may not even be aware that such learning has taken place! He is merely doing what is psychologically *efficient,* seeking rewards where he finds them.

Our task, then, is to provide *attention and other rewards for non-anxious behavior.*

Emphasis is now on the *half-full* glass, a positive attitude, and selectively rewarding the child when he is competent, assertive, and non-fearful in the presence of potentially frightening events. Let's go back to Mary Ellen and her father and see how this is done:

Dad has given Mary Ellen the suggestion that she get angry at witches. She does this and experiences some success. Yet some of her anxiety remains. The next time her father asks her to go into her room and prepare for bed, the following dialogue ensues:

MARY ELLEN: Dad, I'm too scared of the witches to brush my teeth.

FATHER: Still a bit afraid, honey?

MARY ELLEN: Yeah.

FATHER: Well, sometimes it takes time for scared feelings to go away. But I'm really proud of how well you're doing, becoming the boss over those witches.

MARY ELLEN: The boss?

FATHER: Uh huh. In charge. You know how to be the boss, don't you?

MARY ELLEN: By getting mad.

FATHER: That's right. If you start to feel scared, you know what to do. You can handle it. Now go get ready and when you're through, we'll work on that puzzle together.

If Mary Ellen persists, or goes to her room and returns a few minutes later without having prepared for bed, her father should avoid a lengthy discussion, repeat his suggestion, "You can handle it," and give her a reward (his attention) *after* she has completed her assigned tasks. While it is important to allow the child to express feelings about a traumatic event (channels of communication should be left open), to constantly inquire, "Are you okay?" or "Are you still scared?" is not beneficial.

There are other rewards, besides parental attention, that can be given to a child for masterful behavior. These will differ from child to child depending upon likes and dislikes but can include money, outings, games, and privileges. We will examine the use of specific rewards as well as how to *fade them out* (for we don't need to pay a child forever to sleep in his room!) in the following chapter.

Children Are Their Own Best Therapists

Children have a special ability to help themselves deal with fear. Aided by their well-developed sense of fantasy and imagination and lack of defensiveness about looking "silly," they unknowingly make use of therapeutic principles in a natural and spontaneous manner. So subtle are these self-help methods that they often escape our attention.

The practice of *repeated viewing* is common in children and it is a natural form of desensitization: the child wants to keep seeing the same scary movie until he feels in control. He is able to do this at his own pace, because while in the theater, he is free to close his eyes during the most frightening parts. In addition, while he may have been taken by surprise by certain scenes the first time he saw the movie, by the second time he will be prepared for them and thus more in control. It is difficult to get too worked up over the shark in *Jaws* once you've seen the film twelve times! (One of my patients did, in fact, see *Jaws* a dozen times. By the last viewing, he regarded the movie as little more than light comedy. Satisfied with his conquest of the Great White Shark, he went on to other victories.)

Children may not be able to say exactly *why* they want to see the same film, or TV show, time after time. It is as if they are driven by a natural instinct for self-help. They will continue to expose themselves to what frightened them, unless stopped by well-meaning adults, until they feel in control.

In addition to the desensitizing properties of repeated exposure, the activities that take place during movie viewing can be therapeutic. You'll remember that we listed eating and drinking as good "enemies" of anxiety. Children love to nibble popcorn and sip soft drinks, and most theaters make more money from their concession stands than they do from the price of admission. The next time you go to the movies, you might notice how brisk the business is at the refreshment stand when a frightening feature is playing.

Children also prefer to attend movies in groups. They sit together, giggle, and make wisecracks. Often, to the dismay of other viewers, these jokes are blurted out at particularly tense moments, and this is no coincidence. These youngsters are using humor—and group support—in order to fight feelings of anxiety. It is group therapy of the most natural kind, although a little inconsiderate.

If we take a look at the children's stories and nursery rhymes that have endured from generation to generation, and from country to country throughout the world we'll see that there is a common theme of *violence or threat*. In many instances the threat is to the child directly. In *Hansel and Gretel*, the witch attempts to eat the two main characters. In other stories and rhymes, an animal or grown-up is the victim, as in the case of the *Three Blind Mice* who get their tails cut off. Some other examples are:

Snow White: The young girl is almost poisoned.
Three Children on the Ice: A trio of youngsters fall into a frozen lake and are never seen again. At the end of this nursery rhyme, parents are urged to take better care of their children.

Little Black Sambo: The child comes close to being devoured by tigers.

Rock-A-Bye-Baby: "When the bough breaks, the cradle will fall and down will come Baby, cradle and all!"

Little Miss Muffet: A girl is terrified by a spider.

Goosey Goosey Gander: "I met an old man who wouldn't say his prayers; I took him by the leg, and threw him down the stairs."

Jerry Hall: "He was so small, a rat could eat him, hat and all."

Bye-Bye Baby Bunting: The child is abandoned by his family. (And not to be forgotten are *Humpty Dumpty, Jack and Jill, Cinderella,* and countless others.)

Don't be surprised at the somewhat gruesome content of stories and rhymes you recall with nostalgia. It is precisely *because* nursery rhymes and fairy tales deal with threatening themes that they have endured.

What do children do with nursery rhymes? They *repeat* them. Over and over again. While skipping rope, in pleasant gamelike contexts, or in groups of friends. They repeat them until the rhymes have lost all of their meaning, and, thus, all of their fear-eliciting properties. Until they are harmless.

And fairy tales? The child may read and re-read them himself, at his own pace, or he may have Mom or Dad read the story out loud, in a warm secure setting. This enables the child to experience something that has the potential to frighten him in such a way that he learns to master his anxiety and feel in control.

Most of us have never thought of protecting our children from nursery rhymes or of censoring their fairy tales. Why? Because, we ourselves have repeated these poems and stories so many times that they have lost any semblance of threat for us. And that is exactly what we need to let our children do.

To a child's mind, one good way to deal with something frightful is to *become* that thing. Identification with the aggressor helps explain the fascination that children appear to have for the bizarre and the spooky. If little Gordie can become Frankenstein, then he need never be bothered by the monster again.

Children can identify with the aggressor through play-acting rituals. For example, two youngsters at play may solemnly divide up roles, so that one is the Good Guy, the other the Bad Guy (This is of course the central theme behind Cowboys and Indians, and Cops and Robbers). The Good Guy then proceeds to get rid of the villain. Next the roles are reversed. Finally everyone has been the Bad Guy and there's no need to be afraid of him.

Another common identification with the aggressor takes place during holidays such as Halloween. Children don costumes and become Dracula, the Wolf Man, or the Wicked Witch for one night. The fact that this is often done in groups strengthens the anxiety-reducing, funlike quality of the experience. Most parents have noticed the glee with which children strive to become as frightening and ghoulish as possible on Halloween. It is the joy of being in control.

Nightmares

Children, like adults, take their worries to bed with them. If they crawl under the covers feeling extremely tense, anxious feelings may lead to nightmares. In fact, fear and anxiety often express themselves most strongly during sleep.

When children dream, their minds run free. Even youngsters who are old enough to understand that it is impossible to fly have no trouble seeing themselves soar through the air like Superman in a dream. While dreaming, the child can change size, shape, and color with utmost comfort. He can talk to imaginary characters and experience them as very real. He can see, hear, touch, and smell in a distorted manner without sensing anything out of the ordinary. In other words, the child's already strongly developed sense of fantasy becomes even stronger during the dream state. Because of this, relatively minor fears can be magnified and blown out of proportion while dreaming.

Children may have nightmares for reasons other than anxiety, of course. There are certain physical diseases that result in disturbed sleep. Some youngsters have bad dreams after eating certain foods or following a particularly active day. Such nightmares almost always fade away quickly and require no special attention.

Bad dreams are not the only symptoms of nocturnal anxiety. The child who wakes up complaining of a sore jaw may be grinding his teeth as he sleeps. Several experts have expressed the opinion that bedwetting can be the result of increased tension during certain stages of slumber. Sleep walking and sleep talking have also been cited as examples of nighttime tension. But nightmares are the most common childhood sleep disorder.

Normal Nightmares

It is not unusual for children to have bad dreams as often as three to six times a month. Parents may be unaware that a child is experiencing nightmares because the child sleeps quietly and the dreams fade rapidly when he wakes.

Some children may remember nightmares and want to discuss them. The best parental policy in these cases is calm reassurance and allowing the child to talk about what's on his mind.

It is unwise to make a fuss over occasional bad dreams. Undue focus upon something that is normal can raise the child's anxiety about sleep, transforming a series of isolated bad dreams into a chronic pattern of sleep disturbance.

When nightmares are *persistent* and *repetitive*, however, it is wise to examine the child's daytime experience for evidence of stress. If bad dreams occur every night, or several times during a night, for more than three weeks, I would consider this persistent. If the same dream repeats itself over and over, something is on the child's mind. A physical examination is then in order. If this proves normal, and the nightmares do not appear to be tapering off, it is time to look for psychological factors.

Nightmares Versus Night Terrors

There are two main types of bad dreams that children experience. First are *common nightmares*. These take place, as do pleasant dreams, during a *light* stage of sleep called *rapid eye movement*, or, REM sleep. During REM nightmares, the child may lie still or he may thrash around a bit. He will remain sleeping or he may wake completely and remember that he had a bad dream. REM nightmares occur in children of all ages and they are similar to the bad dreams that adults experience.

There is a second type of bad dream that is quite different from the common nightmare. It occurs as the child comes out of *deep* sleep and is a disorder of arousal (waking) rather than sleep. It is called a *night terror* and can alarm parents if they are unprepared for it.

The unique characteristics of a night terror are:

1. The child sits up or walks around. There is a good deal of movement associated with true night terrors.

2. The child screams quite loudly or may talk emphatically and rapidly.

3. The child cannot be wakened. His eyes may be open but it is almost as if he is in a trance.

4. The child falls back asleep and has *no memory* of having had a night terror.

Night terrors are most common in children under the age of six. They may occur in older children or adults but this is quite rare.

We are not sure what causes this disturbance of arousal.

Some experts feel that children who are *very deep sleepers* are particularly susceptible to night terrors as well as to *bedwetting* and *sleepwalking*. It is not unusual for the same child to present two or even three of these symptoms.

Opinion is also divided as to whether night terrors are purely physical, psychological, or both. My own feelings are that while certain children may be prone to develop such problems, it takes psychological stress to bring about recurrent night terrors. In every case of this problem that I have seen, there has been something frightening in the child's life prior to the beginning of the symptom. And psychological treatment has been very effective in reducing and curing the disturbance.

I have described night terrors in detail because I have seen how they can distress unprepared parents. Even doctors, unfamiliar with the pattern that night terrors take, can become unduly alarmed and further raise parental anxiety.

In most cases, night terrors do not last long and go away without any sort of treatment.

If night terrors persist, a psychological approach should be taken. Such was the case with five-year-old Brian, who was brought to my office because neither he nor his parents had gotten a good night's sleep for several months.

Brian had been left with his grandmother while his parents went out for the evening. There was an old "Dracula" movie on television, and Grandma let Brian watch it. That night, he had a nightmare. His parents comforted him and thought little of the matter until the next night, when the bad dreams occurred again. When the nightmares persisted for a week, Brian's parents began to get concerned but then, just as abruptly as they had started the dreams stopped.

Several weeks later Brian came down with the chicken pox. During a high fever, he began to hallucinate—claiming that he saw Dracula in front of him and screaming in terror. After that, despite the fact that he was over the chicken pox,

Brian's nightmares about Dracula started up again and got progressively worse, occurring several times a night. Bedtime became a fearful, tense period for the entire family. Brian's parents, feeling frustrated and helpless, took him into their bed and let him spend each night there.

Soon Brian began to act fearful and withdrawn during the day, and was increasingly reluctant to leave his mother's side. On top of this, apparently connecting his grandmother to his anxiety, he refused to have anything to do with her, to the extent that he was unwilling to talk to her over the phone.

Brian underwent a complete physical from his pediatrician, who found nothing wrong and referred the family to me.

When I asked the parents if Brian ever spoke about Dracula during the day, they told me that soon after the nightmares had started he had expressed a desire to buy a Dracula costume—cape, mask, and teeth.

"Of course we refused," his father informed me. "We saw what one exposure to Dracula did and we certainly didn't want any more problems."

Was there a connection between chicken pox and the development of the nightmares? I believe there was.

When he was ill, Brian ran high fevers. This is not unusual in childhood illness, and some youngsters run temperatures as high as 105°F—a temperature that would be considered dangerous in adults. Such fevers are often accompanied by hallucinations—which can be terrifying because they seem so real. In Brian's case, a hallucination of Dracula re-ignited his previous fear of the mythical vampire and made it more intense. Illness weakened his resistance to both physical and psychological stress and the night terrors began again. Obviously, Dracula had been on Brian's mind all along but had been suppressed. The febrile hallucinations served to bring him to the surface. The fear generalized so that the mere mention of "Dracula" brought about anxious feelings in Brian. Since he had viewed the frightening film at his grandmother's house, he associated *her* with his negative feelings and refused to visit her or even talk to her. Having seen the film at night, he began to develop fears of the dark and anxiety about going to bed. Learning by modeling also took place. Brian's parents, upset by their son's symptoms, reacted with anxiety. They became noticeably tense as evening rolled around and Brian, sensitive to their moods, immediately picked up on this. His parents' tension served as a cue for the boy's own distress. Seeking to protect him, they quickly switched off the TV when any potentially frightening material appeared on the screen. In this way they communicated to their son: "There really is something to be afraid of on that screen."

As the nightmares continued and bedtime developed into a nightly trauma, the boy's parents took him into their bed. At this point, learning by payoff began to play an important role. Brian found himself getting more attention from his parents than he ever had before. Moreover, he got to snuggle up with them in bed, lying, literally, in between them.

In confronting this unfortunate set of circumstances, I took a cue from Brian's desire to buy a Dracula costume. Though his parents refused this request, believing it best to protect him, had they complied they might never have needed to come to my office!

By asking for the costume Brian was saying: "I want to become Dracula in order to master him. *I want to be in control.*" Of course if anyone had asked him if this was the case he would have been puzzled and confused. *Without being consciously aware of it, this five-year-old boy was trying to develop an effective treatment plan for himself.*

The treatment plan which we devised for Brian gave him another chance to gain control over Dracula. Here is what we did:

   1. I advised Brian's parents about the importance of mod-

eling and coached them in giving him "You can handle it" messages. They were told to allow Brian to regulate the TV himself. If he felt something on TV was too frightening he was free to walk away from it. If he felt like watching, that was all right, too.

Brian's mother and father were advised to stop making a fuss every time he spoke of being frightened. Instead, they placed a comforting hand upon his shoulder and told him, "Dracula isn't real. You can handle him."

2. In my office I guided Brian to become angry at Dracula rather than afraid of him. Together we drew pictures of the vampire. I coached the boy to say things like "I'm mad at you, you rotten bum!" until he was comfortable doing this by himself. The pictures were torn up with growing fury and tossed in the wastebasket. Brian was advised to do this any time he started to feel just a *little* afraid of Dracula. He was given the explanation that he couldn't be mad and scared at the same time and that being mad got rid of feeling scared. I also made a point of telling him, "You can be the boss over Dracula. You can be in charge."

3. Due to his nightmares Brian had developed an inappropriate nighttime habit—sleeping in his parents' room. As we all know, habits are hard to break, and it is often best to proceed gradually. Because of this, no attempt was made to have Brian sleep in his own room right away. During a discussion that included the boy, his parents, and me it was decided that Brian's goal for the first week was to sleep anywhere in the house except in his parents' bedroom. His mother and father were advised to be firm in not allowing him to seek refuge with them and were prepared for the strong possibility that Brian would cry when refused admittance to their room. On the morning following a night of appropriate sleep Brian was to be rewarded with a nickel.

At this point it may be useful to discuss the question of

rewarding or paying a child for good behavior. Some parents feel uncomfortable about "bribing" a youngster.

Actually, bribery is not an accurate description for this kind of reward system. Bribery implies something that is underhanded, dishonest, and used to undermine justice. Rewarding appropriate behavior, on the other hand, when done in an honest and forthright way, is what good child-rearing is all about. The child with a long-term psychological problem often has one or more habits that are not useful for him to maintain. He has been rewarded in the past—with parental attention and special consideration—for doing things that are not good for him. Therapy means reversing that learned process.

A common parental objection is: I can understand rewarding a child for doing what is good for him, but I'm uncomfortable about using money. Why can't I just give him attention?

The answer to this is that while praise given for appropriate behavior can be effective if efforts are made to offer it consistently, *using a tangible reward*—something the child can see, feel, and touch—*helps speed up the therapeutic process*. This is because children think in concrete rather than abstract terms. Adults need concrete rewards too—how many individuals would continue to work simply for job satisfaction if the salary check stopped coming?—but they are especially important for children.

When choosing a reward, be sure to sit down with a child and ask him what he likes—what is rewarding for *him*. Parents are sometimes surprised to find that their perceptions of what the child enjoys are quite different from his.

Though Brian was only five years old, he was included in our discussion as a full, participating member. He was told that sleeping outside of his parents' room was something that should be rewarded because this was his job, and we knew it was a hard one. In choosing his reward, he selected money. And in determining the amount of money to be paid for each "good night" he came up with a nickel. (Children usually respond fairly when they are sincerely given the chance to decide upon a specific monetary reward. When their estimates are too high, a bit of good-natured negotiation almost always solves the problem. Parents and children who cannot eventually agree on something like this need to examine their communication pattern. In such cases, professional help is desirable.)

I anticipated that Brian might continue to feel fearful at night despite the fact that he had been shown how to make the fear go away by being angry. Therefore, he was given a "menu" of other things he could do in order to make himself less afraid:

He could turn on his radio.
He could turn on his night light.
He could go to the refrigerator and get a drink.
He could draw a picture.
He could *not* go into his parents' room.

Brian was instructed to choose items from his menu whenever he felt *just a little* afraid. Quite often children will wait until their anxiety reaches a high level before trying to do anything about it. This sets up failure rather than success. The key is to not allow anxiety to grow so intense that it cannot be mastered.

The next week Brian and his parents reported the following sequence of events:

On the first night Brian became afraid after being put to bed. He walked to his parents' room, tried to gain entry, was refused, and threw a tantrum in the hall. His mother found it hard to keep from relenting and allowing him to come in. His father, however, helped her remain firm. Brian fell asleep in the hall, had a nightmare, but was rewarded the next morning with a nickel and praise. This first night represented his "testing the system"—trying to see if his parents really meant business. Fortunately, he saw that they intended to be firm. Despite his resistance, he was comforted by their consistency.

The second night he slept on the couch in the living room. When he began to feel afraid, he got mad at Dracula. No nightmare.

The third night he slept on the couch. No nightmare. And so on. . . .

I praised all the members of the family for following through and gave special tribute to Brian for having been the "boss over Dracula."

During the second week, Brian's goal was to sleep in his room—not in his bed, but *anywhere* in his room. This flexibility made him feel more in control. Once again, each morning following a "good night" he was to receive five cents along with praise from his parents.

As he had during the first week, Brian tested the system. He slept in the living room and protested energetically when he didn't receive his nickel the next morning. For the next six days he slept in his room. No nightmares occurred.

The goal for the third week was extended so that Brian had to sleep in his room *twice* in a row in order to receive five cents. During the fourth week this was stretched to four days in a row. By the time Brian and his parents came for a two-month follow-up appointment his job was to sleep a whole week in his room for one nickel. The nightmares had not come back during this period.

At this point Brian announced that he no longer wanted to be paid for sleeping in his room and that he felt he was handling things quite well. (He was!) He had earned quite a bit of money and felt like spending it now. His parents and I agreed, and we praised his progress.

That week Brian took his earnings, went with his mother

to the toy store, and purchased a Dracula costume, complete with cape, mask, and fangs.

I've remained in contact with Brian's family. He continues to make strides socially and academically. He has no nightmares. Once he sent me a greeting card upon which he had drawn a fanciful representation of Dracula. The card was in honor of the birth of my son and in it Brian advised me to make sure that the newborn didn't end up being afraid of the vampire. I thanked him and assured him that I would do my best.

It is not always necessary to embark on treatment or therapy in order to get rid of a pattern of night terrors. One good example of this comes from a story related to me by a colleague who knew of my interest in sleep disorders. This psychologist recalled that one of his sons had begun to experience night terrors—complete with screaming, the trancelike state, and no memory of the event—at the age of four. Perplexed and worried, the boy's parents took him to several doctors, none of whom could understand why the nightly episodes were occurring.

Then, one night the child's mother listened carefully to what her son was saying as he sat shaking, in the midst of a night terror. She heard him screaming about wolves and the "wolf house." She could clearly make out his terrified refrain:

"No wolf house! No wolf house!"

She mentioned this to her husband, and to him the cause of their son's distress became clear. The family had been considering moving to a new home. One of the houses they had contemplated buying was owned by a family with the last name of Wolf. Apparently, the child had overheard his parents talking about going to see the "Wolf house" and had taken this to mean that the family was going to visit a den of wild animals! Unable to communicate his worries to his parents, he took them to sleep with him.

Both parents sat down and explained to their son that no real wolves were involved in their real estate transaction. Following this explanation, the nightmares disappeared.

This story points out several important things. First, it is valuable to *observe* carefully what goes on during a nightmare. In particular, the content of what the child actually says during his bad dreams can point out what is bothering him. This is the power of constructive, active listening.

Second, young children have a tendency to take things literally. Given a rather narrow life experience, the four-year-old child interprets "wolf house" to mean one thing, and one thing only. When parents understand this tendency to think in absolutes, they will attempt to explain things clearly, simply, and on the child's own level.

The quick "cure" experienced by this child illustrates how important it is to explain major changes to children so that they are *prepared*. When the family plans to buy a new home for instance, even if it means only a move down the block, children should be given ample time to prepare themselves psychologically for the shift. To some extent, all change—even that which is seen as positive—can be stressful. And no one hates "bad surprises" more than children do—because not knowing makes them feel helpless.

The cases of Brian and the boy afraid of the "wolf house" indicate that both children were reacting fearfully to something temporary and short-lived. Neither Dracula nor wolves had to be dealt with on any long-term basis. But what of the child who is faced with ongoing, long-lasting stress and reacts with disturbed sleep? In most cases, professional help is necessary, and we will discuss this in more detail in this chapter and in the section on illness and hospitalization. Even in instances where the source of anxiety is apparently permanent, parental attitudes can be important factors. The case of Christie illustrates this.

A few days after her second birthday, Christie was diagnosed as having leukemia. Once a disease that meant almost certain death, leukemia can now be controlled and managed medically so that most children who develop it live for several years and some are cured. In order to treat leukemia, however, medical procedures that are painful or uncomfortable must be used, and most children with this disease experience continuing distress.

Christie was no exception. She received chemotherapeutic drugs that made her hair fall out and caused her to feel ill. She underwent frequent injections, spinal taps, and bone marrow tests. Nevertheless, her leukemia went into remission—it disappeared. No one was sure if this meant that the little girl was cured, or if the disease would eventually return. Despite this uncertainty, Christie's parents and her doctors were quite pleased with her medical progress.

At the age of two and a half, she began to experience night terrors—as many as six a night—every night. She was examined for possible medical causes for this problem and none were found. When, after several months, the night terrors did not go away, she was referred to me for psychological consultation.

It was clear that she had experienced considerable stress due to her medical treatment. This was supported by the fact that during her night terrors she screamed out "Don't hurt me!" and "Christie doesn't want hurt!" Of all the medical procedures that she had to undergo, her mother reported that one particular test—the bone marrow aspiration—seemed to upset her the most. (This procedure involves puncturing the hip bone to get a sample of marrow, and it is commonly done with all children who have leukemia. Despite the fact that local anesthesia is used, most youngsters report it is a distressing experience.)

Christie's mother shared her daughter's fear of bone marrow tests. Her own anxiety made it difficult for her to be at Christie's side while the child underwent the procedure. She could tolerate watching her child go through blood tests and injections, but bone marrow tests were too much for her to bear, so she left the room when they took place.

Complicating matters was the fact that, like Brian's parents, Christie's mother and father had also begun to take the little girl into their bed at night each time she had a night terror.

Children below the age of six are especially concerned with *separation*—with being abandoned by their parents. In fact, the way in which young children express their anxiety is often with statements such as "Don't leave me!" or "I want my mommy!" For Christie, the anxiety of experiencing a painful medical procedure was increased by the fact that *she went through it alone*.

We devised the following treatment plan: As was true with Brian, Christie had been rewarded with parental attention for inappropriate sleep habits. In order to reverse this harmful payoff, she was no longer taken into her parents' bed after having a night terror. Instead, during a dream, her mom and dad went into her room briefly, and reassured her with the statement "Mommy's [or Daddy's] here."

Unlike Brian, the source of Christie's fear was not something "imaginary" or temporary. She was going to have to experience bone marrow tests for years to come. Nevertheless, there were things that could be done to help her gain more mastery and control over the situation. She was presented with a Raggedy Ann doll, needles, cotton swabs, and bandages. At first she was too frightened to touch these objects, but she did watch, wide-eyed, as I performed the bone marrow test on the doll.

Eventually, her courage grew and she was able to touch the medical apparatus. She became comfortable holding the equipment. Finally, after several sessions, she was able to "play Doctor" and administer a series of angry bone marrow tests to the hapless Raggedy Ann. I encouraged her to express any feelings "the doll" might have, including anger, fear, and hurt. Her parents were shown how to help her do this at home.

Being a medical patient means giving up a certain amount of control and submitting while others do things to your body. This can be especially frightening for a child because it causes emotional helplessness. When the child "plays Doctor," he assumes the *role* of the person who is in charge, and experiences feelings of being in control. This type of mastery allows him to view the medical procedure from a new point of view. We have discussed how children attempt to be the person or thing that frightens them in order to feel in control. Brian wanted to be Dracula. And Christie needed to be the doctor.

Allowing Christie to puncture the doll repeatedly also helped because it opened up a flood of angry feelings. This anger was incompatible with anxiety.

After I explained to Christie's mother the importance of separation fears, she agreed to try to remain with her daughter during bone marrow tests. She was given breathing and muscle relaxation exercises to help her.

During Christie's next bone marrow procedure, her mom stayed with her. Everyone noticed that the test went much more smoothly. In the past, the little girl had been withdrawn and depressed for two or three days following the procedure. But this time, once the needle had been withdrawn, she got up from the table, smiled, walked around, and had a good appetite.

During the following week, she experienced her first night in months without bad dreams. As a way of showing her how pleased they were with this, her parents took her for a hamburger and milkshake at a favorite fast-food restaurant. Gradually, she began to sleep through the night more and more often. Each time, this was rewarded by a morning-after treat. Christie's parents were careful not to imply that she was to blame when she had a bad dream. But they did let her know that they were happy when she slept peacefully.

During treatment, careful records were kept of the little girl's sleep pattern. When we examined these charts, we found that there was a definite increase in night terrors just before bone marrow tests. This confirmed our initial guess that what we were seeing was an anxiety reaction to medical stress.

It took Christie longer to get rid of her nightmares than it did Brian. This was because the stress to which she was exposed was much more intense and *repetitive*. Nevertheless, after two months, and despite the need to undergo bone marrow tests, she was sleeping peacefully. Her leukemia did not come back, and she is, as of this writing, a happy, well-adjusted child.

In a case such as Christie's, where the child is beset by long-term stress, professional help is necessary. No amount of expert advice will be useful, however, unless parents actively participate in the treatment plan. Christie's mom and dad learned how to reward appropriate sleep instead of giving her attention when she had problems. They were able to stand by her during times of pain and stress. This helped her overcome strong feelings of separation anxiety. They became skillful at aiding their child in expressing her feelings—and they made all the difference in the world.

5

Insomnia

Nightmares interrupt peaceful sleep. But what of the child who finds it difficult to fall asleep in the first place? If no medical reason is found for the problem, psychological factors should be explored.

Bedtime Power Struggles. All too often, putting a child to bed turns into a nightly power struggle. The more the parent demands that the child go to sleep, the harder the youngster resists. There may be a repeated pattern of cajoling, threats, temper outbursts, and punishment—with a miserable time had by all. Ironically, the child may be so worked up by the time he reaches his mattress that he finds it difficult to relax and has genuine difficulty sleeping.

Some children are what I call excellent *self-regulators.* That is, they virtually discipline themselves. They eat when they are hungry and stop when they are full. They "listen" to their own bodies so that when they feel tired, they yawn, announce that they are going to bed, and trundle off without debate. Other children, however, need some sort of structure imposed from the outside. The setting of bedtimes is important for them, because children are much more secure when they are given a schedule within which to work.

It is important to understand, however, that while children benefit from having a reasonable bedtime—a specified hour at which the day's activities begin to draw to a close—*it is unrealistic to expect them to fall asleep on demand.*

Achieving sleep depends upon specific changes within the brain. In order for slumber to occur, the electrical circuitry—as measured by brain waves—of the central nervous system must prepare itself. Children, like adults, do not go spontaneously from being wide awake to sleep. There is a transition stage in between, a presleep stage. The speed at which presleep gives way to actual sleep varies depending upon levels of relaxation, fatigue, physical health, and individual differences.

One thing about going into presleep is clear. It requires a *passive* psychological state. In other words, you cannot try to fall asleep. You must let sleep happen to you. In this sense, sleep is a paradoxical process. Countless insomniacs have reported various methods of trying to achieve slumber, all of which fail, because *the harder you try to sleep, the more awake you become.*

Parents who tell children ''I expect you to be asleep in five minutes'' are not only demanding something unreasonable, they are defeating their own purpose. This type of demand makes the child feel anxious and the more anxious he becomes, the harder it is to sleep. On top of this, such ''orders'' openly invite rebellion.

Children also resist going to sleep when it is presented to them as a kind of punishment. Going to bed can represent being excluded from favorite activities—being literally kicked out of the family room and exiled to the bedroom.

The child who is not particularly anxious or afraid but who resists going to sleep has usually been *systematically rewarded for inappropriate sleep behavior*. He has received attention for stalling, delaying, arguing, and not complying. Though the type of attention that such behavior generates is not particularly pleasant from a parent's point of view—for who enjoys threatening and arguing?—to a child, *even negative attention is preferable to being ignored*. Parents who want to reverse this negative learning pattern need to make sure that the child receives positive payoff for appropriate nighttime behavior. How can this be done?

First, going to sleep should never be used as punishment. On the contrary, parents need to turn bedtime into something that the child looks forward to. This means that the actual time set should be reasonable. If it is too early, the child will not be physically ready—in terms of fatigue—to sleep and will merely lie in bed angry and frustrated. In addition, while parents should remain firm about specific bedtimes, firmness should be tempered with reason. If there are ten minutes left before a favorite television program concludes, it is wise to let the child finish even if this means going ten minutes past bedtime. Not doing so creates needless, time-consuming power struggles that will most certainly last longer than ten minutes.

In order to prevent the child from feeling that by going to bed he is being "left out," parents should spend time with him as a consequence of his cooperation. This can include accompanying the child to bed, spending a few minutes in pleasant conversation, reading bedtime stories or making them up, or playing games of short duration. Bedtime can be one of the most cherished of childhood memories, a period at the end of each day when parent and child relax together and enjoy each other's company. Such "good time" needn't be long—ten or fifteen minutes can be quite meaningful. And it is certainly less time-consuming than the usual half-hour arguments over going to bed.

Besides being reasonable and flexible, bedtime rules should be explicit and completely understood by both parent and child. In one family, the bedtime routine may call for Dad to spend fifteen minutes telling Emily bedtime stories. In another, both parents may chat with Daniel. In a third, Mom and Jennifer may play two games of checkers.

Parents should guide the child toward choosing bedtime activities that enhance the onset of sleep. These involve fantasy, concentration, relaxation, and can, preferably, be conducted in bed. Some children enjoy being rhythmically stroked on the forehead or arm and this seems to make them feel relaxed. Others benefit from listening to music. The tradition of bedtime stories is an excellent one though, unfortunately, it is becoming a thing of the past due to television.

Once the time allotted for bedtime activities has drawn to a close, parents should be firm about leaving the room. Most children will "test the system" at one time or another— bargaining for one more story or one more game. At this point, the thing to do is to say goodnight, offer a kiss, and leave the child to find his way to sleep. Dim the lights and suggest a message similar to the following:

"You can stay in your room with the lights low [or off]. After a while you may find yourself getting more comfortable and wanting to go to sleep. And that will be fine."

Most children, having already become drowsy during the pleasant bedtime period, will readily comply and fall asleep within moments of a parent's leaving. Others may test limits and work hard at staying up. Such last-minute power plays usually last no more than one or two nights and parents should ignore them. In response to stall tactics, such as the child coming repeatedly out of his bedroom and asking for water or the answer to a suddenly pressing question, etc., the best thing to do is to propel him, firmly but *without anger,* back to his room. Avoid arguing or giving attention to such behavior. Once children see that their parents mean business, they will follow through. It may be necessary to lead the child back to his room several times until he gets the message. Again, this should be done without anger; what the child needs in this type of situation is parents who are calm, rational, and able to offer him structure and discipline. Though they may gripe, most children *want* discipline because it offers them a sense of stability and safety.

Up to this point we have been concerned with delayed sleep that occurs in the absence of unusual fear or anxiety—except for the tension that is generated by bedtime power struggles. There are times, however, when sleep is hampered due to the existence of worries, upsets, and conditioned fear. This is true insomnia.

Fear-induced Insomnia. When anxiety prevents the child from falling asleep, it is a situation similar to that found in nightmares. The difference is primarily one of timing. In the case of bad dreams, anxious feelings express themselves after sleep has begun, while in insomnia, tension prevents the onset of sleep.

When faced with an anxious child who is insomniac, the first step is to try to find out what is bothering him. It may be something that responds to parental reassurance and comfort, as in the case of the boy with the "wolf-house" fear. One especially common anxiety that keeps children up at night is worries about grades, peer relations, and the like. Since parents are usually very concerned about their children's school performance, it may be hard for them to discuss such worries and remain calm. Let's consider the following scenario:

MOM: Is something bothering you, Jeremy?

JEREMY: [reluctantly] I've been a little worried.

MOM: About what?

JEREMY: Uh, about school.

MOM: What about school?

JEREMY: I got into a fight with Michael and the principal said if it happens again we'll both get our grades lowered.

MOM: The principal! You were sent there for fighting? Who started it?

JEREMY: He did!

MOM: You're sure?

JEREMY: Yeah! Honest. He started it!

MOM: Well, I told you not to hang around Michael. If I hear of any more troubles with fights, no more television for two weeks. Is that understood?

JEREMY: [dejectedly] Uh huh.

MOM: Are you sure?

JEREMY: I said yes!

MOM: All right. Now go to sleep.

It is clear that Jeremy has not been rewarded for honestly expressing what is bothering him. What has started out as mother's attempt to find out why he has been having trouble sleeping has ended up as an exercise in courtroom interrogation. Not only will Jeremy be less likely to talk freely to his mother about his feelings in the future—for he has been soundly punished for this—but his inability to sleep will most certainly intensify.

Before bed is not the time to get into detailed discussions of misbehavior or arguments about school performance. Such conversation is best relegated to a time of day when everyone is alert. Parents who find out that their child's insomnia is the result of school-related worries need to offer comfort and reassurance. Losing sleep can only harm future academic performance. If the child *wants* to talk about what is on his mind he should be encouraged to do so. But don't try to solve any large-scale problems just before lights-out. There are few school-related problems so important that they cannot wait until morning. Jeremy's mother might try the following approach in response to her son's telling her about his fight:

MOM: It sounds like getting into trouble really bothered you.

JEREMY: Yeah. It wasn't even my fault.

MOM: You'll probably be more careful in the future.

JEREMY: Uh huh. I will.

MOM: I can understand your being bothered, but you don't have to let it keep you up. We can talk more about it if you want, or we can wait until some other time. It's up to you.

JEREMY: I don't feel like talking about it now.

MOM: That's okay. It's all right for you to feel comfortable and want to sleep.

In this exchange, Mom has granted Jeremy permission to relax. She has also suggested that he feel relaxed and that he will be able to handle troublesome situations in the future. Children are highly influenced by messages from important people in their lives. Parents can use this for the child's benefit.

By allowing Jeremy to express what is on his mind, his mother rewards him for the process of communication and helps him relax at the same time. This will make it easier for him to fall asleep.

When children present repeated insomnia due to unresolved anxiety, the next step is to take action to help them unlearn the fearful associations that are hindering their slumber.

The same behaviors that can be used to dispel anxiety in children suffering from nightmares can be utilized with youngsters whose tension prevents them from falling asleep. A relaxed atmosphere is crucial. Reassuring activities might include snacking, drawing, coloring, playing brief games, listening to music, using a night light (which can be gradually reduced in wattage and eventually faded out), and being told bedtime stories—particularly those which encourage flights of lighthearted fantasy.

Do not put the child insomniac into a bedtime situation where he must make narrow choices. It is better to say something along the following lines:

"Your goal, the way I see it, is to learn to stay in your room at night and to see how much fun that can be. I don't care if you sleep or not. Just stay there and have a good time. If you want to sleep, you don't even have to do it in bed. You can sleep under the bed. Or on the window sill. Or standing on your head or anywhere else you can think of. Of course, if you choose to sleep in your bed, that's okay too."

My patients usually react with smiles and laughter to this sort of explanation. The humor helps reduce their anxious feelings about going to bed. Something that seemed tremendously scary takes on a slightly ludicrous air. In addition, because they are offered several choices about going to sleep in terms of location and position, their feelings of helplessness are reduced. When you don't *have* to stay in bed, bed begins to look a lot more comfortable.

I also stress that the child should call on his personal anti-fear "menu" *as soon as he feels just a little afraid.* In order to do this, the child learns to identify how fear affects his body. In one youngster it may begin as butterflies in the stomach. In another, tightening of the scalp and shoulder muscles. Being more aware of the "early warning signs" of anxiety means being able to fight fear when it is at its weakest.

Guided Imagery

One good way to help children—particularly young ones—to relax before bedtime is through the use of *guided imagery,* a method of helping the child imagine pleasant fantasy scenes that are incompatible with anxiety. In order to make maximum use of children's natural affinity for play, guided imagery should be presented in terms of a game—The "Imagination Game."

The Imagination Game is best played in the child's room with Mom or Dad sitting by the bedside. The lights should be dimmed or out. This activity should be carried out only if the child is willing and enthusiastic.

The parent should speak in a calm, soothing tone. The game should be honestly described as a way that Mom or Dad can help the child to see some nice things, have a good time, and feel more comfortable. The child's ability to see these things by himself should also be stressed.

There are as many variants of the Imagination Game as there are children—in fact many more. Some children will enjoy seeing themselves take a space trip with a favorite super-hero, others will marvel at the experience of riding a horse or swimming or playing baseball. Rely upon your knowledge of your child's preferences and experiences in constructing a pleasurable fantasy. Often an unstructured approach can be taken, as in the example of the *Favorite Place Game.*

In this game the child is in bed with lights dim or out. Parents can sit at the bedside and may touch or stroke the child. Soothingly, the parent instructs the child to:

1. Think of a favorite place. Somewhere you really would like to go. Maybe it's somewhere you've had a good time. It can be a place you've already been [name an amusement park or some other place the child obviously enjoyed] or somewhere you'd like to go.

2. Close your eyes if you want to.

3. Take a deep breath. Good. Now another one. Good. Now continue to breathe comfortably.

4. Now think of your favorite place, again, and see yourself going there and having a good time. You can go by yourself, or with someone. [Pause] You can tell me about it or you don't have to.

At this point, if the child begins to narrate where he is and what he is doing, the parent can gently enhance his imagery. For example, if he says he is going to Disneyland, the parent can suggest that he see the entrance gate, describing it in detail, along with other familiar sights, talking reassuringly, softly, and sparingly.

Some children may not speak at all but it will be quite obvious from their even, slow breathing and peaceful facial expressions that they are having a marvelous time.

After two or three minutes of imagery, the parent can continue:

5. You can stay in your favorite place and have a good time, feeling more and more comfortable [or: relaxed, feeling good, feeling happy, etc.]. I'm going to go into the other room and I'd like you to stay here and continue to have a good time for as long as you choose.

Many children will fall asleep soon after engaging in guided imagery. There should be encouragement to practice the Favorite Place Game. I often given the following explanation:

"Going to a favorite place is just like riding a bike. The more you do it, the better you get. Each time you can see new and different things, or you can continue to enjoy the same special place."

As with the sleep avoider, the child with anxiety-induced insomnia has learned a pattern of inappropriate nighttime behavior; he is rewarded with parental attention for delaying, stalling, or having a problem. Because of this, the parent should make a conscious effort to avoid *prolonged* periods of time at the child's bedside—periods that go beyond the mutually agreed-upon bedtime routine. For example, the Favorite Place Game can be played in five to ten minutes and children can learn to develop their own images with less and less parental guidance over time.

Appropriate presleep behavior should be rewarded with praise. In cases where poor nocturnal habits have become solidified, I strongly suggest the use of tangible rewards.

1. *Parent and child agree upon behavioral goals.* These should start out at a level that ensures success and doesn't create "forced choices." For example, the child who has made a habit of sleeping in his parents' room for six months will have difficulty breaking this habit "cold turkey" and going straight into his darkened room. The first week's goal might be that he sleeps anywhere *but* his parents' room. The next week this could be modified to sleeping in his room with a night light. And so on. The key is *specific definitions* of goals. *The rules need to be clear.*

2. *Written performance records are kept.* An ordinary calendar can be used in which the child records each time he achieves his nightly goal.

3. *Successful behavior is rewarded.* The child can be given a token, such as a poker chip of his favorite color, the morning after each successful night. At the end of the week, these tokens can be redeemed for specific rewards. The nature of these rewards should emerge from discussion between parent and child. In one case this might mean money. In another, a predetermined number of tokens can be used to purchase a trip to a favorite place or extra time with Mom or Dad. For young children, delaying gratification is difficult. They

should receive rewards after each successful night and shouldn't be expected to wait for an entire week. Praise should be used in conjunction with concrete rewards.

4. *Tangible rewards are faded out.* As the child progresses in learning new nighttime habits, more is expected of him. This can be presented to him in a complimentary way: When you were little, it was great for you to crawl. Then you got bigger so you started to walk. Now you know how to run. The same thing is true with your sleep. You're doing so well that you're expected to do a bit more.

Whereas the reward system may start out with one token for each night of appropriate behavior, the next week it can be "thinned out" to two nights per token, and so on. Don't move on to the next step until a consistent pattern of success has been established at the previous level.

Quite frequently children will voluntarily state that they no longer wish to receive payment for handling things well. The satisfaction of gaining mastery is enough for them. This is a truly hopeful sign that a troublesome pattern of learning has been reversed.

Moving from Crib to Bed

Children may resist making the transition from crib to bed. While many youngsters look forward to sleeping in a "big kid's bed," others, particularly those who are feeling insecure, may long to keep the status quo. For example, children who are faced with a new sibling sometimes regress—return to behaviors appropriate for younger children—in an attempt to compete with the baby. Having the child give up his crib at this time may be particularly difficult. It is better to discuss this with the child prior to the baby's arrival and to emphasize the positive aspects of sleeping in a big bed. ("You can get up by yourself and get toys in the morning." "You can get up and get a drink if you're thirsty.'') For the youngster who continues to resist, a one-week period of grace may be advisable. During this hiatus, the child may decide to move to the bed himself. If he doesn't, a reward system should be instituted: Parent and child chart appropriate behavior—in this case, sleeping in the appropriate place. Each morning following a successful night, the child should be rewarded with something he likes. When a full week of spending the entire night in his own bed has been established, the rewards should be faded out. Praise should always be paired with the concrete reward.

While there is no "official" age when children should make the shift from crib to bed, most youngsters feel comfortable making the transition by two and a half. Some children will request a bed prior to this age, or will crawl out of the crib. The child who is attempting to gain voluntary control over his bladder at night will need to sleep in a bed that he can leave easily to go to the bathroom.

In the case of the child who continues strongly to resist leaving the crib, possible factors in his environment that are causing him to feel insecure should be examined.

School Avoidance

Beginning school is a momentous occasion in the life of the child. The onset of schooling often represents a first exposure to prolonged separation from parents. The reactions that children display in response to this are varied. Some children will show little or no separation anxiety and will be enthusiastic about beginning an "academic career." Others will exhibit overt fears of abandonment—clinging to parents, crying and fussing when it is time to go to school, and generally putting up a vigorous protest. The majority will fall in between, behaving in an ambivalent manner.

School may be thought of as the child's work. It is the place where he acquires both academic and social skills and prepares for adulthood. Like any work situation, the scholastic environment is fraught with both positive and distressing experiences. Children have a natural curiosity that makes learning inherently pleasurable. On the other hand, being in school

91

often means that the youngster will be exposed to greater structure and discipline than he has been accustomed to. He will also be placed in extended contact with his peers and may have to bear the brunt of teasing and bullying. The shy child with little prior social experience can find this particularly painful.

Despite the emotional difficulties that can accompany going to school, it is important for children to face these experiences and develop coping skills. Carrying the work analogy one step further, it is safe to say that youngsters who remain absent from school for extended periods are markedly similar to unemployed adults. In fact, researchers have found that such children frequently display symptoms of depression and anxiety. The school-absent child reacts negatively to being cut off from contact with intellectual and social stimulation.

Prolonged school absence is a form of isolation.

The challenge, then, is to provide support and comfort to help the new student deal with some of the rough spots while firmly encouraging him to maintain regular attendance.

Preschool Separation Anxiety

There is a current trend to send children to school at younger ages than ever before. It is not uncommon for youngsters to be sent to preschool at two and a half years. Several factors contribute toward this new emphasis.

Women may be motivated to continue or begin professional careers. Mothers who choose to remain at home may desire time for themselves, sending the child to nursery or preschool several hours a week. There has been an encouraging trend for fathers to become more involved in child-rearing, allowing both parents to work part-time and share time at home with the children. However, this remains the exception rather than the rule and financial needs increasingly dictate that both parents acquire full-time jobs. Thus, in many cases, separation of two-, three-, and four-year-olds from their parents is a fait accompli. Our goal is to find ways of minimizing the child's trauma.

The first step is selecting the right kind of preschool. Very young children do not profit from an environment where academic skills are stressed or where they are subjected to overly rigid patterns of discipline. Parents should be wary of nursery schools that stress teaching three- and four-year-olds how to read, write, and do arithmetic. Early academic "enrichment" of the middle-class child has few provable long-term benefits—children not offered such preparation catch up quickly, so that by the end of first grade there is no discernible difference in the learning skills of those who have been "prepped" and those who have not.

The young child has a right to enjoy the precious years of early childhood free of academic pressure. He will, most likely, face twelve to twenty years of education once grade school begins and will undergo more than his share of performance anxiety.

Children love and need to play and they do not require adult intrusion and structure in order to do so. Left to their own devices, they will invent marvelous games and experience the psychological enrichment that results from doing what comes naturally. The ideal preschool is one that provides a safe, secure, and physically pleasant setting within which the child can engage in self-discovery, both by himself and—if he chooses—with other children.

Preschool administrators who boast of how they are able to elicit advanced academic performance from their young charges are not operating in the best interests of the child; they are appealing to the parents' sense of vanity. (What parent doesn't secretly harbor the wish for a child with extraordinary talents?) Preschools that put too much emphasis on such words as "teach," "instruct," "train," and "structure" are highly suspect from a psychological point of view. Ironically, youngsters who have been exposed to several years of rigid academic pressure before first grade can develop learning problems in elementary school because they are "burnt out"—fatigued and overworked at the age of six. These children also run the risk of losing much of their natural creativity, because creativity flourishes in an atmosphere where curiosity, novelty, and diversity are encouraged. Too much structure is its mortal enemy.

Obviously this does not mean that a child who expresses the desire to learn to read or write before the age of six should be refused the opportunity to do so. The very fact that he takes the initiative to ask for this type of stimulation indicates that he may be ready for it. But no child below the age of six should be *coerced* into becoming a premature student.

Once a suitable preschool has been found that stresses warmth and fun and provides for the physical safety of the child, the second step is to explain to the youngster why he is beginning a new life routine. Make sure he understands that he is not being sent away as a punishment or because he's done something wrong. Children can benefit from realistic explanations of Mommy's need or desire to work and from reassurances that they are still loved. It may be necessary to repeat such explanations several times.

It's important to take the child for one or more visits to the preschool *before* he actually enrolls, so that he has a chance to adapt gently to new surroundings in an atmosphere of low pressure and in the company of his mother or father. A good nursery-school teacher will make a special effort to help the new child feel welcome and will have the psychological sensitivity to let him move at his own pace. When this does not occur, it is a warning sign that this particular preschool should be avoided. In fact, any time your instincts suggest that something isn't quite right about the preschool or the people who run it, follow those feelings and *don't enroll your child.*

On the first day the child attends preschool, it is advisable for the parent to remain with him, perhaps for nearly all of the first day, although this is by no means necessary for all children. Parental presence can be tapered off so that by the end of the first week, separation can take place after a few minutes. The thoughtful preschool teacher will help in this process by offering the child pleasurable new experiences that enlist his attention. Parents should clearly let the child know that they will be coming back for him. This should be done in a concrete, specific way. A three-year-old cannot grasp the abstract concept of two o'clock, but he will be able to understand "I'm coming to pick you up right after sandbox play." It is, of course, essential to follow through on such promises and be punctual.

Despite a gradual approach, some youngsters will continue to protest when the parent leaves. Give the child two or three weeks to adapt to his new surroundings. Be sure to spend time with him at home at the end of the day; allow him to express his feelings and reassure him that you love him.

In cases where symptoms of anxiety persist for several weeks and the child shows no sign of adapting to a well-run preschool, he may simply not be ready for this type of separation. Such youngsters may prefer to stay at home with a warm, consistent baby sitter. A familiar one-to-one relationship seems to suit them better than does a school setting. For this type of child, another try at preschool six months later may prove more successful.

Acute School Anxiety

The most common type of school "phobia" occurs in the child of six or seven who is attending first or second grade.

Quite frequently resistance to going to school takes place on a Monday, or after the child has been absent from classes due to a minor illness. The avoidance reaction can range from a stubborn angry refusal to go to school, to manifestation of psychosomatic symptoms such as flushing, dizziness, nausea, and vomiting.

Such acute school anxiety occurs in psychologically well-adjusted children. It is an *over-response*. By this I mean that it represents an exaggeration of a normal behavior.

Most children attempt to get out of going to classes from time to time. It's just more fun to stay home and watch television and play than it is to sit in class and do schoolwork. The child who has been home for several days in a row becomes especially aware of the benefits of being out of school and is likely to try to prolong his vacation for a while. This is why post-illness periods are high-risk times for this problem.

In trying to avoid school, children will use many tactics, including crying, pleading, and malingering. Youngsters who have received much attention in the past for being ill, are likely to use physical symptoms as heavy artillery in the Monday Battle of Independence. Even after having arrived at school, they may complain to the teacher that they are not feeling well. This often results in a trip to the school nurse, who will then call the parent and tell him or her to pick up the child and take him home.

Acute school avoidance is one of the few anxiety-related problems that *should not be handled slowly or gradually*. Arguing or debating with the child about his need to go to school should not take place. There should be no attention paid to delay tactics. The youngster whose health has been verified by his pediatrician should not be allowed to avoid school but should be told, firmly, that he has to go to school, that it is his job to do so, and that this is not an issue that is open to debate. If necessary, the child should be led to the schoolyard gate and deposited on the school grounds. Parents should make it clear to school administrators and teachers that they expect him to remain there and do not wish to be called to take him home. To the question "But what if he says he doesn't feel good?" they should answer: "He can feel bad as easily at school as he can at home."

There has been a marked change in attitudes of school personnel toward truancy and absenteeism. In the past, teachers were quick to inform parents of their responsibility to educate their children, and truant officers were very real people whose job it was to enforce the laws governing school attendance. Today, there is a tendency to shift responsibility for academic matters from school to parents. At times, teachers, principals, and school nurses seem more than happy to release the child who complains of vague symptoms after only a cursory checkup. There is no doubt that today's schools are troubled institutions and that teacher morale is understandably low. However, since there is little that parents can do about this in the short run, they will need to be assertive in enforcing the rules of attendance.

Each day that the physically healthy child is permitted to be absent makes it harder for him to readjust to school routine. As he avoids responsibility, his anxiety level is likely to rise. The secondary gains that come from staying home are potent and must be combatted with quick action.

If typical schoolyard cruelties—teasing, bullying, and ridicule from peers—are discovered, there is little that a parent can do other than offer sympathy and support. Except in cases where a child's physical well-being is threatened, it is unwise to intervene or try to patch up peer conflicts.

There is only one way that I know of to get rid of teasing behavior. And that is to ignore it. Most children tease, and most are teased. Teasing is a special kind of power play. The payoff that comes from ridiculing someone else is the loss of control that the victim exhibits in terms of an angry or frustrated response. The object in teasing is to "get to the other guy" or make him "lose his cool" (translation: lose emotional control). By removing the payoff for teasing, we *extinguish* such obnoxious behavior.

This sounds simple, but there is a catch: extinction does not take place immediately. Rather, habitual behavior for which a reward is suddenly removed tends to *increase at first,* then decrease until it finally drops out.

Consider the example of two eight-year-old boys, Gavin and Sean. Each day Sean torments Gavin by calling him a "nerd," "weirdo," or "jerk." Gavin responds by getting angry and calling Sean a name in return; in general, he rewards the other boy by losing control. Then Gavin is advised that if he ignores Sean, the teasing will stop. Full of hope, he goes to school and struggles to remain oblivious to Sean's taunts, only to find that the teasing not only continues but also gets worse. Frustrated and furious, Gavin gives up, breaks down, and the old pattern continues.

Such initial increase of teasing occurs due to a "maybe-the-next-time" phenomenon. Put yourself in Sean's place. You have been consistently rewarded for teasing, when suddenly your reward—getting to the other guy—stops. Your first thought is: *I'll keep trying. Maybe the next time Gavin will give in.* Maybe-the-next-time thinking is also responsible for the rapid and enthusiastic behavior exhibited by grown-ups operating slot machines in Las Vegas. When no money comes out the first time, the gambler doesn't give up. He thinks, "Maybe-the-next-time I'll hit the jackpot," and keeps cranking the handle. As with Sean, it will take an extended period of no-payoff for him to abandon the game.

Knowing this, Gavin can successfully extinguish Sean's teasing behavior. He will be prepared for the fact that at first Sean will tease longer and stronger but that if he sticks to his guns and doesn't pay any attention to it, Sean will finally give up and go elsewhere for payoff. This entire process may take a few days or it may take weeks, but time is on Gavin's side if he sticks to his guns.

Children can be helped to endure the period between the time they first begin to extinguish teasing behavior and when it finally stops if the power struggle can be presented as a game. One such game is the Science Experiment. In the following dialogue, nine-year-old Jeanine's mother explains the Science Experiment to her:

JEANINE: And Kathy called me an ugly slob and made fun of me.

MOM: It sounds as though you feel really bad about that.

JEANINE: She stinks!

MOM: You know, Jeanine, I was teased when I was your age.

JEANINE: You were?

MOM: Yes. Nearly every kid gets teased. Daddy was teased and so was Uncle Ken.

JEANINE: Daddy got teased!?

MOM: That's right. When you're teased it doesn't mean there's anything wrong with you. Kids can always find something to tease about. It can be your hair or your eyes or your name. Or being too tall or too short. Or having too many freckles, or not having any. It doesn't matter. Everyone gets teased about something.

JEANINE: Well, I don't like it.

MOM: There is a way you can stop Kathy from teasing you . . .

JEANINE: What's that?

MOM: By ignoring her. When she teases, she wants you to get mad, so don't give her what she wants.

JEANINE: But that's hard!

MOM: Yes, it is, but it's the only way to stop teasing. The secret is to make believe that you're a scientist and Kathy is a monkey that you're experimenting on. You've got to look at her but not let her know that you're studying her.

JEANINE: Kathy looks like a monkey.

MOM: Well, then that should make it easy for you to pretend.

JEANINE: Ha. I'll be the scientist and she'll be the monkey.

MOM: Now, it's important for you to know what's going to happen when you start to ignore Kathy. She's not going to stop right away. In fact, she's going to tease you *more*. Do you know why?

JEANINE: Cause she's mean?

MOM: No. Cause when you stop getting mad, she's going to figure that she needs to tease you *harder* to get you mad. So at first she'll keep trying and say to herself, "Maybe the next time I tease Jeanine she'll get mad. I'll keep trying." But what will you do?

JEANINE: Keep on ignoring her?

MOM: Exactly! Just remember that you're the scientist. You're in charge of the experiment. Keep on ignoring old monkey Kathy and watch what she does. You might even want to secretly write down how many times she teases you—you know, keep a science notebook.

JEANINE: Yeah! That'll be fun. A secret science notebook.

MOM: If you keep on ignoring her when she's mean, she'll finally give up. Because she'll learn it's not fun to tease Jeanine. Maybe she'll start to tease someone else or maybe she'll just give up on teasing. I don't know. But she won't have to bother you anymore.

In the beginning of this dialogue, Jeanine's mother helps

her daughter to express her feelings about being ridiculed. Then she lets her know that being teased is normal and in this way attempts to reduce feelings of guilt and stigma. Telling her that people she admires—Mom, Dad, and a favorite uncle—have gone through the same experience, helps further to weaken Jeanine's sense of being different or strange. Rather than punishing herself by *internalizing* another child's taunts, Jeanine comes to see teasing as an unpleasant but inevitable part of growing up.

Mom goes on to explain the principles of extinguishing teasing behavior to Jeanine and prepares her for the initial increase in teasing. Placing the extinction process in the context of a game serves a multiple purpose. By playing the role of an authority figure (the Scientist), Jeanine is helped to feel sufficiently in control to endure the difficult days ahead. Keeping secret records provides distraction from the taunts.

When the insults begin to reduce, Jeanine will experience additional emotional satisfaction. Having written evidence of her progress will make this clearer to her. At this point, it will be easy for her to keep on ignoring Kathy. The trick is to help her get to this stage.

Techniques such as the Science Experiment—and creative parents can develop their own variations of the game—can be used for any child who is exposed to ridicule for one reason or another. Using extinction, the youngster learns to confront a situation that is anxiety provoking rather than avoid it. He also learns to develop healthy control over the abusive behavior of others, a skill that will come in handy throughout his life.

School Failure and Test Anxiety

Another major cause of school-related anxiety in children is experiencing failure in one or more subjects. The word "failure," as used here, is totally subjective and depends upon the child's and family's expectations. For one youngster, anything above a D is considered adequate, while for another, a grade below A is considered total failure.

The child who has had a history of academic problems may have a learning disability due to perceptual, motor, familial, or psychological factors—or a combination of these. The topic of learning disabilities is a complex one and cannot be covered in this book. Our discussion will be limited to the youngster who, having performed at a satisfactory level, *suddenly* begins to show signs of failure. In such cases, anxiety is very often an important contributing cause.

Lowered school achievement is common in children undergoing long-term stress such as divorce and parental illness. Anything that upsets the child's psychological equilibrium or disrupts his usual life pattern can lower his ability to concentrate, as well as affect his motivation for academic achievement. Psychological counseling to help him express his feelings and develop methods of coping with stress can be very useful.

The child who has been a scholastic success can become traumatized when he is faced for the first time with subject matter that is hard to understand. This frequently occurs when a youngster is first exposed to mathematics. Having never had any academic difficulties before, the child is ill-prepared to handle things that don't come easily. His anxiety rises and this further affects his ability to comprehend and concentrate. As his performance drops, a deep sense of failure may set in. This can be particularly devastating for the child whose family puts great emphasis on academic excellence. Rather than face parental anger or disappointment, he bottles up his feelings and the cycle of anxiety and failure continues.

It is one thing for parents to maintain expectations of success and standards of achievement, and quite another to place a heavy burden of academic pressure upon a child. The youngster who is terrified of failure is ill-equipped to deal with the realities of life and its inevitable frustrations. The sooner a child learns that it is okay to make mistakes—there are erasers on pencils for a reason—the better he will cope with imperfections in himself and other people. Apart from the inhumanity of excessive pressure, rigid expectations are not *pragmatically* wise. Parents who are heavily concerned with academic achievement need to understand that anything that raises anxiety to extreme levels is likely to bring about failure rather than success.

The child experiencing sudden school failure may be in need of extra academic help. Achievement testing in the school or by a private psychologist often helps to clarify exactly in what areas he requires tutoring. *Parents should not attempt to tutor their own children.* Such endeavors nearly always fail. The most brilliant mathematics professor is likely to have great difficulties explaining the fundamentals of long division to his or her own child. Objectivity is lost and the teacher-pupil relationship is overcome by the much stronger and deeply emotional parent-child bond. This applies to athletic as well as intellectual activities. Many of us are aware of the difficulties experienced by the child whose father coaches the Little League baseball team. Tutoring is a job for a professional who is hired specifically for that purpose.

There will be children who are academically prepared and who fully comprehend the subject matter of a specific class, but who nonetheless do poorly on exams. This is the result of *test anxiety*. Such youngsters may complain of being ill just before the test; they feel dizzy, have nausea and queasiness, and go to the bathroom frequently. Often diarrhea is experienced. The child who is test-anxious feels especially frustrated at knowing the material and then "forgetting" it, or "freezing up'' in a testing situation. Because anxiety weakens memory and concentration, the effect it has upon test performance is very real.

Test anxiety in children will sometimes respond positively to parental statements of reassurance and support. The child needs to know that how he does in school is only *one small part* of who he is and that his parents love him no matter what grade he gets in a specific exam or class. Activities at which he is succeeding need to be stressed and feelings of guilt, shame, and failure must be minimized. Parents should avoid doing things that indicate undue concern about taking tests, such as constantly asking "How did you do?" or "Did it go better?" Such behavior is an indication of parental anxiety which the child will surely model.

When faced with a test-anxious child, parents need also to examine their own expectations and behavior regarding competition, success, and failure. Are they perfectionists? Does dinner-table discussion constantly center around who does what the best? Is calling someone stupid the ultimate family insult? Such attitudes are modeled and quickly internalized by children who apply these standards to themselves.

When test anxiety persists in the face of a warm, supportive family atmosphere, brief psychological therapy can be very effective. Such treatment, carried out by a qualified child psychologist, involves building of rapport, helping the child express his feelings and clarify the source of his anxiety, and teaching him relaxation or imagery exercises that desensitize anxious associations related to being tested. Frequently, successful therapy can be carried out in less than ten sessions.

Chronic School Avoidance

In contrast to children with acute school avoidance who are almost always psychologically well-adjusted and trying to prolong a vacation, there are older children, usually eleven years and above, who develop a slow-growing, rather insidious pattern of absenteeism accompanied by extreme anxiety. This problem commonly manifests itself during the last years of elementary school or during junior high.

The chronic school avoider may begin by complaining of physical symptoms or may appear emotionally agitated. Despite the fact that no medical symptoms are found, he will often be able to convince parents to allow him to stay out of school for several days. Then he may return, only to stay out the following week. Gradually the periods of absenteeism get longer while the days in school grow fewer and fewer, until a definite pattern of truancy is established. Such children can become quite hysterical when asked to return to school.

The majority of chronic school avoiders are suffering from psychological problems in addition to their anxiety about school. Parental alcoholism or illness, intense marital stress or divorce, frequent moves, financial problems, or an abnormal child-parent relationship are frequently present in the home-lives of these children. Poor patterns of family communication are also a factor. Sometimes a clear history of parental over-protectiveness and overemphasis upon health and illness is found. Chronic school avoiders and one or both of their parents may also show signs of hypochondriasis.

This learned pattern of maladaptive withdrawal should be treated in the same manner as acute school anxiety. The child should be immediately returned to school and prevented from further experiencing the side benefits of atypical behavior. Such rapid treatment is often hampered, however, by the fact that parents of chronically school-avoiding youngsters are themselves ambivalent about school. They may collaborate with the child, consciously or unconsciously. Until such parents are able to resolve for themselves the importance of school attendance, progress is not possible.

Chronic school avoidance thus is a disorder that almost always requires professional psychological help. Therapy should not postpone the child's returning to school but should serve as a cushion for the feelings of anxiety that have been strongly learned. The treatment of choice in such cases is often not individual psychotherapy but, rather, family therapy aimed at correcting maladaptive patterns of communication.

Even Sick Kids Need to Go to School

A special type of school avoidance can occur in the chronically ill youngster, whose disease and treatment interfere with the normal, day-to-day activities of growing up. Included in the chronic disease category are children with heart problems, juvenile rheumatoid arthritis, diabetes, cystic fibrosis, kidney disease, lupus, colitis, congenital bone defects, asthma, hemophilia, anemia, and certain types of cancer.

Chronically ill children may develop avoidance reactions to school for several reasons. First, there is an understandable tendency on the part of some parents to shelter and protect a sick child. They may see him as fragile and unable to handle everyday responsibilities competently. One major aspect of a parent's role is to provide protection. The diagnosis of a major illness in a child threatens the parents' ability to offer such protection and can make them feel powerless. This can lead to heightened parental anxiety and restrictions on the child that go beyond what is medically necessary. The vast majority of children with chronic diseases are psychologically normal and able to cope with everyday life. The child with diabetes and hemophilia can learn to administer medication to himself, through injection. The youngster with cystic fibrosis, by adhering to a schedule of medications, exercises, and diet, maximizes his changes of good health. Children with heart disease, kidney disorders, and most types of cancer can work around the medical restrictions imposed upon them by their disease and maintain normal lives.

Parents of chronically ill youngsters should ask the child's physician exactly what changes in activity must take place to ensure the child's physical safety, and must *avoid imposing restrictions that go beyond this.* In most instances, regular school attendance can be maintained. For example, among the hundreds of young cancer patients with whom I have worked, less than 1 percent have had to stay out of school on a permanent basis. In exceptional cases, programs of home tutoring and special education have been arranged, but only as last resorts.

Parents may have to take the initiative in returning a chronically ill child to normal, classroom attendance. Most school systems are not prepared to handle the needs of the seriously ill child and are afraid of harming him. Like parents, teachers may relax their standards and overprotect the sick child. This is insulting; the youngster feels that because he has a certain disease he is no longer considered competent and therefore nothing is expected of him. If a teacher is worried that a child might fall sick in the classroom—and such mistaken attitudes regarding many childhood diseases are common—he or she will be reluctant to make academic demands. Parents, guided by the child's physician or other health professional, need to provide the school personnel with realistic information and make it clear that they want him to be treated as normally as possible.

A second cause of heightened school anxiety in chronically ill children stems from the physical changes that can result from disease and treatment. Steroid drugs can cause short stature and puffy "Cushingoid" facial features. Chemotherapy often causes hair to fall out. Certain diseases of the joints cause noticeable malformations and limping. Radiation can darken the color of the skin. Children, particularly adolescents, can become self-conscious and suffer from lowered self-esteem. Looking different can also make the ill child more vulnerable to taunts and teasing. Despite this, the chronically ill child needs to be strongly encouraged to return to school and face this problem rather than avoid it by withdrawing. Once the child has explained to his classmates why he looks different, the teasing usually stops. In the case of persistent riducule, extinction techniques such as the Science Experiment game can help.

Some diseases and treatments require that the child be hospitalized for prolonged periods. Many pediatric medical centers minimize inpatient care and encourage more and more home treatment, but there will be times when certain children are forced to miss school due to hospitalization. This can cause the ill youngster to fall behind academically and raise his already heightened anxiety about returning to school. Keeping in close touch with the child's teacher so that he can be supplied with class and home assignments is helpful. Many pediatric hospitals have teachers on staff whose specific job is to aid in this process.

I have emphasized the importance of the academic experience for chronically ill youngsters because school, with all of its problems and flaws, is the contemporary American child's *normal environment*. Removing him from that environment reduces his chances of growing up psychologically well-adjusted. Some seriously ill children have normal life expectancies, others do not. Most live for several years. The choice is between making those years profitable by providing the child with challenges and opportunities for academic and social growth or allowing him to withdraw from life and experience an impoverished state of minimal survival.

The hardest part of meeting this challenge comes initially

when the child's resistance to demands and responsibilities is high and when parental anxiety can weaken usual standards of discipline. Once the initial trauma has been dealt with, most youngsters with chronic disease adapt well.

Going to the Doctor and the Dentist

Medical and dental visits are likely to be repeated experiences for most children. Such encounters—even checkups—are potentially stressful because they are often associated with pain or discomfort. Having his body probed, disrobing, tolerating hypodermic injections, and being asked to urinate into a jar are just some of the procedures that the child is apt to find anxiety provoking. In addition, since many children are taken to the doctor primarily when they are ill, not feeling well can quickly become associated with the medical setting. The way that we handle these visits to health professionals can have a major influence upon how the child copes with them.

There are several steps that parents can take to minimize medical anxiety.

Be Aware of Your Own Feelings About Medical Visits

When a mother or father takes a child to the doctor, ample time exists for the youngster to observe how his parent reacts. Anxiety—even anxiety that is not verbally expressed—will be picked up easily, for children are exquisitely sensitive to the emotional messages transmitted by their parents.

For the parent, simply being aware of his or her own anxiety about medical experience may be enough to help reduce and control these feelings. Motivation to help the child can override previously learned patterns of fear.

Adults who wish to take more direct steps to reduce anxiety can try the following relaxation exercise:

Brief Muscle Relaxation

The goal of brief muscle relaxation is learning to recognize the difference between tense and relaxed muscles so that a deep state of comfort can be rapidly achieved.

1. Sit in a comfortable chair with feet flat on the floor and arms at your side.
2. *Slowly,* take a deep breath and exhale. Repeat three times.
3. Continue to breathe *slowly, rhythmically,* and *comfortably.*
4. Imagine a pleasant scene, such as a day at the beach, a hike through the mountains, or a swim in a beautiful lagoon. Maintain this image.
5. Continue to breathe comfortably.
6. Tighten both hands into fists, until the knuckles turn white. Hold for a count of five.
7. Slowly open both hands and relax them, just letting them spread open. Concentrate upon how heavy,

warm, and relaxed they feel. Maintain relaxation for a count of twenty and allow it to continue.

8. Extend both arms straight in front of you and tighten them, as if they were planks of wood or pieces of steel. Hold tightly for count of five.

9. Slowly let arms drop to your sides, limp, heavy, and comfortable. Maintain for count of twenty and allow relaxation to continue—being aware of feelings of relaxation spreading through your entire body.

10. Repeat the tighten-loosen procedure (tighten for count of 5, relax for count of 20) for the following body parts: Both feet, both legs, abdomen, chest, and back.

11. Still breathing comfortably, tighten muscles of the face for count of five and slowly allow them to relax and feel comfortable.

12. Now your whole body can be relaxed. If any tension exists in a muscle, repeat the tighten-loosen exercise until that muscle feels comfortable.

Maintaining this feeling of comfort, think about taking a trip to the doctor for a checkup. Start your imaginary trip at a point where you feel relaxed; perhaps this involves getting into your car and driving from your home to the doctor's office, or starting at a point before or after that. Keep breathing slowly and comfortably. Continue the imaginary trip to the doctor. When you begin to feel the least bit anxious, *stop*, think of your pleasant scene, relax your muscles, and when you are comfortable, continue. Soon you will be able to imagine more and more of the trip and feel comfortable doing so.

Practice brief muscle relaxation before you go to sleep and when you wake up in the morning. Each time you will feel more deeply relaxed and achieve comfort more rapidly. Once you are familiar with the steps—usually after one practice session—do brief muscle relaxation with your eyes closed.

If you are actually scheduled for a doctor's appointment, use this relaxation exercise before and during the appointment. If at any point you begin to feel anxious, stop, tell yourself the word "Relax," loosen your muscles, and think of your pleasant scene. If the anxiety surfaces in the pit of your stomach, tighten and loosen your abdominal muscles until they are totally comfortable. If your head begins to ache, work on the muscles of the forehead (by raising and lowering your eyebrows) and face.

Of course, it is particularly important that you be relaxed on the day you take your child to the doctor. Parents who remain anxious about medical stimuli should not attempt to reduce their child's fears without professional help.

Help the Child Develop Trust

Nothing infuriates physicians, dentists, and nurses more than to have a parent admonish a child with a statement such as, "If you don't behave, I'll take you to the doctor and he'll give you a shot." One office nurse described such behavior as "sending the child into the ball game with two strikes against him."

Children do not visit the doctor because they have misbehaved. To tell them otherwise is dishonest and reinforces the child's natural tendency to blame himself for illness. Because young children do not always have clear ideas about what causes things to happen, they are likely to feel responsible for all sorts of things over which they have no control—including being sick. Such mistaken thinking, though quite normal, can bring about considerable guilt, if reinforced.

Increased guilt raises anxiety. Pain and anxiety are positively related—the guilty, anxious child can actually *feel more pain* while undergoing injections and blood tests. In addition, if the child perceives the doctor as an instrument of punishment, he is likely to be uncooperative, hostile, and distrustful. This can turn a routine examination into a drawn-out nightmare for everyone involved—the child, the parent, and the doctor. Such repeated bad experiences lead to chronic fear. Children should be given accurate explanations for medical procedures such as "The doctor will examine you to make sure that you are healthy" or "The injection you'll be getting is to protect you against a disease called. . . ."

It is essential that the child develop a sense of trust in the doctors and nurses who take care of him. Obviously, some of the responsibility for this rests on the shoulders of the health professional. If a doctor is usually unsympathetic, brusque, and does not take the time to relate to the child, it is advisable to find another doctor. Parents need not sacrifice emotional sensitivity in order to obtain expert knowledge and first-rate medical training; there are many fine physicians who possess all these qualities. In general, children should be cared for by a *pediatrician* specifically trained in both the physical and emotional aspects of child health care. With regard to dentistry, the question is more open. There are some general dentists who enjoy treating children, and standard dental training provides enough expertise for them to be able to do so. Many dentists, however, refer young patients to *pedodontists*—specialists in childrens' dentistry.

When I conduct seminars for interns and resident pediatricians in developing communication skills, I routinely advise them to take the time out to talk to the child and get to know him, when *not doing anything medical to him*. In a few minutes the child can see that the doctor is not always equated with pain and discomfort. Seeing the human side of a physician offers children the opportunity to develop positive associations to doctors and establishes a firm basis for a relationship that lasts for years.

Even the most sensitive doctor, however, can be undermined and sabotaged if he is presented to the child as unsympathetic. Consider two children who visit the dentist for the first time. Both are five years old, and neither has previously experienced dental pain.

Rudy approaches the dental chair with some hesitation. He has noticed, as he and his mother entered the waiting room, how nervous she has become. She fidgets, bites her nails, and doesn't seem to listen when he talks to her. When the two of them are called into the office, his confusion mounts, because although the dentist seems like a nice person, Mom is noticeably upset. When Rudy gets up on the chair she tells him:

"Now sit still, even when it hurts. And don't be afraid."

Rudy wonders what there is to be afraid of.

The dentist examines Rudy's mouth and cleans around the gums a bit. It doesn't really hurt, but each time the dentist turns his back, Rudy's mom is at his side inquiring, "Did he hurt you? You can cry if he did." After a while, Rudy begins to wonder if something is wrong with him because he doesn't feel much pain and his mother seems to think he should. Every time she asks him "Are you okay?" he feels a little more nervous. By the end of the session, still expecting something painful to occur, he is highly anxious. Each time the dentist probes his mouth, he jumps. The dentist grows impatient, and Rudy starts to see that maybe he's not such a good guy after all.

When the cleaning session is over, the dentist remarks that Rudy did a fine job. Rudy's mother says, "He doesn't show it, but I know it hurt him."

During the second dental session Rudy receives a filling. The dentist has to give him an injection of anesthetic which does hurt. Having been "prepared" for this by his mother, who has told him how horrible dental injections are and has illustrated this point with examples from her own experience, Rudy actively resists and fights the needle. The injection takes three times longer than it needs to. The dentist finally has to call in a nurse to hold Rudy's arms down. By the end of the second session, Rudy decides that he hates the dentist. This gives him something in common with his mother and on the way home they have a lengthly discussion about how terrible dentists and doctors are.

Mark and his mother sit in the same dentist's waiting room reading a book together. When he has questions about the dentist, she answers them factually and with details that he can understand. When he inquires why he is going to the dentist, his mom answers, "Dr. Clark is going to meet you and examine your teeth. He will look inside your mouth with mirrors and touch your teeth with tools that look like metal toothpicks. He will probably clean your teeth by scraping them and polish them with an electric toothbrush." Since his mother appears calm, Mark feels little anxiety.

In the chair, Mark's mom asks the dentist to explain to both of them what he is doing. She supplements this with descriptive comments directed at Mark. ("Now Dr. Clark's looking at your back teeth. . . . Now he's checking the front ones.") Her attitude is one of curiosity, rather than apprehension. Mark asks to look at the hand mirror and the dental probes and Dr. Clark obliges. Soon, however, the boy loses interest and starts to get restless. His mother asks him if he wants to hear more of the story in the book they had begun in the waiting room. When he says that he does, she reads to him in a quiet, soothing voice, as Dr. Clark works. By the end of the session, Mark is almost asleep. Everything has gone smoothly. Mark's mom asks Dr. Clark what is in store for the second session, so that she can prepare her son for it.

Both of these cases are true and they illustrate how children can be taught to deal with medical or dental stress in either adaptive or maldaptive ways.

Rudy's mother loves him, yet her anxiety prevents her

from helping him and, in fact, leads him to be fearful. Many adults have negative associations to dentistry. The fact is, however, that the use of modern technology, such as high-speed drills, has drastically reduced the amount of pain that dental patients undergo. Dentistry can be virtually painless. Parents who judge from their own prior negative experiences and emphasize inevitable pain when talking to children about dental procedures run the risk of being inaccurate and needlessly anxiety-provoking.

"Will It Hurt?"

When a child finds out that he is to receive an injection or other discomforting medical procedure, the first thing he asks is:

"Will it hurt?"

In answering this question, keep in mind the importance of honesty and trust.

Never lie to a child about pain.

Parents—and professionals—who say "It won't hurt" when it probably will are committing a grave error. For while the child may believe this the first time, he will quickly feel betrayed and will be less likely to trust the person who lied to him. If a doctor or nurse engages in such dishonest behavior, parents should speak privately to the health professional and inform him politely that the child should be treated more openly. Professionals who react defensively to polite suggestions or refuse to cooperate with such a reasonable request are behaving inappropriately. In such cases, parents should consider switching doctors. Most pediatric doctors prefer to be honest with their patients and may even correct parents who engage in "white lies."

While it is wrong to tell a child flatly that an injection will not hurt, telling him that it *will* hurt can also be inaccurate.

Children have widely varying sensitivities to pain. Some youngsters feel the slightest pinch while others are relatively stoic. Telling a child that he will *definitely* feel pain may "poison the well"—set up self-fulfilling, negative expectations. Some children, who have high pain thresholds and feel little discomfort, may, like Rudy, begin to wonder if there is something wrong with their bodies.

What is the solution to this apparent double bind?

The best answer to the question "Will it hurt?" is:

It can hurt, but it doesn't have to bother you.

This answer is honest but open-ended. It lets the child know that if he feels pain, it is normal, but that if he doesn't, that is also okay. It also imparts a positive suggestion that is therapeutic.

Similarly, if the child asks "How much will it hurt?" a good answer is:

"Everybody feels things differently, but it doesn't have to hurt you a lot."

Prepare the Child for Medical Visits

The child's first awareness that he is going to the doctor should not occur when the family car pulls into the parking lot of the medical office building. As has been mentioned, children hate unpleasant surprises because their feelings of being in control are reduced. All children need to be prepared, emotionally and factually, for medical experiences. They need time to get themselves ready for such events, and the exact amount of time required varies from child to child. In general, younger children benefit from being told an hour or so prior to the visit while older children may want to know a day or two in advance. Once the youngster has had his first visit, it is advisable to ask him:

"How long before we go to the doctor do you want me to tell you about it?"

When the child is unsure, parents can offer several choices: an hour? Three hours? A day? On rare occasions, children may state that they do not wish to be told and, of course, this preference should be honored. Most frequently, they will appreciate being allowed the time to prepare for medical experiences.

In addition to letting them know about the visit, so that they can prepare *emotionally,* it can be helpful to offer children some brief educational experiences, for *behavioral* preparation.

Just as actors gain competence and confidence by practicing their lines, so children benefit from *rehearsal.*

Children prepare themselves on a concrete level using things that they can hear, see, and touch. For example, while most adults turn away during injections or blood tests, most children *prefer to look.* Well-meaning adults who turn the child's head away are doing him a disservice and are acting out their own feelings of anxiety. Looking helps the child to *integrate* and make concrete sense out of the injection. Looking is a means of therapeutic self-education.

One excellent way of preparing children for medical procedures involves the use of a *surrogate,* such as a doll or a puppet. Children below the age of six relate equally well to boy dolls or girl dolls and sometimes even to toy animals. Older children may prefer surrogates that are similar to themselves in age, sex, and appearance.

In using a surrogate, the parent should be familiar with the medical procedure that the child is to undergo. The parent may even need to have observed it at some prior date. The procedure should be broken down into steps and should be described both in terms of *what goes on* (overt behavior) and *how it feels* (emotional content). Inclusion of emotional content is particularly important, since research has shown it to be a crucial factor in reducing anxiety.

Parents can obtain a doll, preferably a soft one, such as a Raggedy Ann or Raggedy Andy, or allow the child to choose a surrogate. The child will often not want to use one of his previously owned toys, because the familiar surrogate has been imbued with its own identity, and the child is reluctant to see it "hurt." Medical apparatus similar to the instruments the doctor will use should be obtained. These can include real syringes (many physicians will allow parents to take home a syringe after removing the needle) or toy ones, alcohol swabs, bandages, etc.

Let us return to Mark and his mother, who are going to the dentist again. Mark has been told that during the visit he will be receiving an injection.

MOM: And Dr. Clark is going to give you an injection right here. [Puts finger in Mark's mouth and presses approximate injection site]

MARK: Will it hurt?

MOM: It can hurt but it doesn't have to bother you, Honey.

MARK: A lot?

MOM: People feel shots differently, but it doesn't have to hurt you a lot. Soon the shot will make your mouth feel tingly as if it's asleep. If you touch it, it won't hurt at all.

MARK: That sounds scary.

MOM: It's okay to be scared, Hon.

MARK: Mommy, I'm scared [begins to look anxious].

MOM: Sometimes there are things we can do to make you feel less scared.

MARK: Like what?

MOM: Well, we can give the shot to Raggedy Andy here so you can see how it's done and you can be Dr. Mark and be the boss.

MARK: And I'll give the shot in the mouth?

MOM: Sure. Watch. Let's put Andy down here on the

table. Now I've got this syringe. Would you like to hold it and look at it?

MARK: Yeah. [Holds syringe, turns it over in his hand, examines it, and makes jabbing motions] "Pow! Pow!" [Giggles]

MOM: [Takes syringe back when Mark has finished looking at it] "First, we get Andy comfortable, lying him down just like this. Now we take this piece of gauze and put numbing medicine on it like this."

MARK: Andy's mouth feels tingly!

MOM: Right. And now we take the syringe and fill it up with numbing liquid called xylocaine from a bottle just like this. And squirt a little out through the top to get rid of bubbles. Then we ask Andy to open his mouth.

MARK: Open your mouth, Andy.

MOM: Good. And now we give Andy the shot of xylocaine right in his mouth. And it can hurt a little so he says ouch, or maybe it doesn't bother him.

MARK: Ouch!

MOM: Now we take the needle out and it's all over. Why don't you try it, Dr. Mark?

Mark's mother will guide her son through the steps of the oral injection. He may ask to repeat the procedure on Andy several times, and she will let him know that he can play Doctor as many times as he wants. During the course of the behavioral rehearsal session, he may jab at the doll and exaggerate the intensity of the injection. This is normal and therapeutic, and Mark's anger will subside over time. We have discussed the value of anger as a counter-anxious emotion and why it is helpful for children to express angry feelings. It is important to allow the child to go through as many repetitions of the preparation as he wants. When children begin to lose interest, this is an indication that they have "worked through" their feelings, for the time being.

The goals of behavioral rehearsal are to acquaint the child with the procedure and to encourage feelings of mastery and control while exposed to medical stimuli. *Parents should not attempt to guide a child through preparation unless they are calm and comfortable about the procedure themselves.*

Many doctors and dentists choose to keep needles and other apparatus hidden from children's view. I do not feel that this is helpful. Certainly such behavior is not based upon scientific data, for research consistently supports the notion that children are better able to cope with experiences for which they are prepared. Allowing the young patient to hold the needle, explore it, and experience a feeling other than anxiety with regard to it—such as curiosity and relaxation—can be highly therapeutic. Health professionals may hide apparatus because of anxiety and guilt about inflicting pain and their subsequent desire to get the procedure over as quickly as possible, or simply because they have been taught to do so. Parents may need to request more open behavior and can emphasize that their child has been prepared.

Doctors should play a role in preparing children by telling them what they are going to do and how it may feel step by step—*before* proceeding. It is helpful to say, "It may feel cold"; "Now I'm going to wipe your arm with a piece of cotton"; or, "Now I'm going to put the needle in, it may sting." If a child asks not to be told what is going on, this should be respected. Most children will want to be informed. Sometimes doctors get so caught up in the procedure that they forget to inform the child or tell him *afterward*. This can be confusing and lead to feelings of betrayal.

Other ways of helping the child prepare for medical procedures include encouraging him to draw pictures of the experience or to make up stories about it. The hero of the story may not be the child, himself, but a make-believe character who represents the youngster.

Behavioral rehearsal may seem time consuming and an overreaction to normal everyday medical procedures. This is not the case. Effective preparation for simple procedures such as injections and blood tests can take place in five to ten minutes, and soon the child will rehearse the procedure with a minimum of parental participation.

Lessening Discomfort

Distraction should never be used as a substitute for preparation, or as a way of concealing from the child what is going to happen to him. Once a youngster has been adequately prepared, there are ways to divert his attention from discomfort. These are, basically, techniques that make use of the "enemies of anxiety" as described in chapter 3.

For example, the use of guided imagery and other fantasy games aids in reducing anxiety (and combating boredom during time-consuming procedures). Mark's mother distracted him with storytelling when he began to fidget in the dentist chair. Children who can imagine going to a favorite place are able to dissociate—disconnect their attention—from something unpleasant and switch to something entertaining. Going on a ride with a favorite fictional character may help a youngster psychologically to "rise above it all."

Doctors and dentists can allow the child to hold and play with a harmless piece of equipment—such as a mirror or tongue depressor—as a reward for sitting still. Of course, both health professionals and parents should use praise as positive payoff for cooperative behavior. While most pediatric doctors offer prizes such as toys and balloons to children *after* the visit, it is much more effective to give these rewards *during* the time the child is in the examining room and behaves appropriately. In this way *cooperation* rather than *escape* is rewarded.

Do not attempt to distract a child who does not fully understand what is happening. A colleague of mine once helped a severely burned eleven-year-old girl tolerate painful changes of dressings by using hypnosis. The child was able to escape into a fantasy world and disconnect her mind from the medical procedure. Nevertheless, when the psychologist visited her patient the following day, the girl refused to speak to her. After gentle encouragement, she was able to say what was on her mind: She felt as if she had missed out on making complete sense of what was happening to her body, despite the fact that she had been spared intense pain! Only after she was able to ask questions and rehearse changing dressings on a doll was there willingness to escape from reality. At that point, hypnosis was successfully reinstated. To this child, feelings of losing control and being manipulated by another person were worse than physical distress.

To Stay or Not to Stay

Most children benefit from having people whom they love and trust remain with them during stressful medical procedures. This is especially true with youngsters below the age of six, for whom separation is a primary issue. Of course in some cases, parental presence can increase rather than decrease anxiety. This usually happens because the parent is modeling anxious behavior to the child, as did Rudy's mother. When a doctor sees that Mom's or Dad's presence is making things difficult for the child, it is quite reasonable for him to ask the parent to leave. The best solution is for anxious parents to resolve their own feelings so that they will be able to support their children. This is what Christie's mom did (chapter 4), and it brought about significant positive change for both mother and child.

Parents who are calm and whose children want them to stay in the examining room should be encouraged to do so. As the child grows older he will want more privacy and may be quite assertive in letting adults know this. It will then be important to let him handle things by himself. The decision for or against parental presence should not be imposed upon the child nor should it be based upon what the parent thinks the child wants. Ask him and respect his wishes.

The parent should not become the doctor's accomplice. There may be times when a child needs to be physically restrained or held down during an injection, for his own safety and so that the procedure can be accomplished. (The probability of this is greatly reduced, however, when youngsters are prepared and dealt with honestly.) Doctors or nurses may request that the parent assist in restraining the child. Such a request can be politely refused. The parent's role is one of supportive resource, not medical assistant. An appropriate answer for the parent would be, "I really don't feel comfortable doing that."

This is not to say that the health professional should be set up as a bad guy against whom parent and child offer collective resistance. Parents should let the child know that they support the doctor and value cooperation with him or her. But they should not participate in the procedure unless failure to provide assistance means the procedure absolutely will not get done (rare, because most medical offices are amply staffed), or when the child himself requests that Mom or Dad assist.

Letting the Tears Flow

A medical procedure is an assault upon the child's psyche and body, despite the fact that it is performed for his own good. Anxious feelings need to be expressed, and one of the most normal and therapeutic ways is through crying. Despite this, children about to cry are often told "Don't cry, you're all right" or "There's nothing to cry about" or "Big boys don't cry."

Grownups' attempts to turn off a child's tears stem from *their own* discomfort at seeing and hearing them cry. This can be true of doctors and nurses as well as parents and other well-meaning adults. In my seminars for pediatric interns and residents, I stress that anyone who plans to spend a significant amount of time with children needs to develop a tolerance for the sound and sight of crying.

Crying is an *emotional release.* Children who are not taught to be ashamed of tears will feel better after having cried. My own research with ill children indicates that youngsters who are able to express their feelings of fear and distress can experience less pain and anxiety during medical procedures than their less communicative peers. If we see crying as a therapeutic behavior and understand that anxiety does not disappear but will be expressed in one way or another, it is clear that trying to prevent crying is potentially harmful for the child. The case of Anthony illustrates this dramatically.

Anthony, a seven-year-old boy being treated with very potent drugs for a medical ailment, was referred for psychological consultation because he developed prolonged emotional depression, withdrawal, loss of appetite, and nervousness before and after receiving his injections. Though some of these symptoms could be attributed to the physical side effects of the medications he was receiving, the fact that his problems began *prior to* taking the drugs indicated that a psychological factor was present.

Another psychologist and I observed Anthony as he received his injections and noticed that he was unusually stoic. In fact, he said not a word to the nurse who gave him the shot but merely sat rigidly, staring straight ahead, turning from time to time to vomit into a basin, literally *suffering in silence*.

Over the next few weeks we got to know Anthony quite well and gained his trust. The other psychologist worked with him directly and I supervised. Gradually, he began to open up and talk about how bad the injections made him feel. He was told that such feelings were normal and that other children had them. Upon hearing this, he began to draw a series of angry, scrawled pictures of a boy—not him, but another child—getting shots and feeling bad. The psychologist went on to tell Anthony that not only was it okay to feel scared and upset, but it was all right to talk about these feelings—to say, "It hurts" or "ouch" or "I'm scared"—and even to cry. It was suggested that he practice these behaviors while undergoing a make-believe injection.

At first Anthony resisted this. He had been taught that it was unmanly to cry and believed that letting the world know how he felt would be acting like a "sissy." Anthony's parents were divorced and the fact that his father was not in close contact with him may have had something to do with the development of such a distorted attitude about masculinity. Sometimes when children do not have a role model for realistic sex-role behaviors, they develop exaggerated attitudes (hyper-masculinity and hyper-femininity). The psychologist who worked with Anthony was male and the boy looked up to him. He was able gradually to change Anthony's attitudes and systematically *trained this youngster to cry*. At first, this took place during make-believe injections, but eventually Anthony was able to go into the treatment room, undergo his shot, and say "Ouch" and "It hurts," as well as let a few tears fall. He was rewarded for this with praise by the psychologist, the nurses, and his mother, all of whom had been informed about the treatment plan.

The results of this training were gratifying. It was as if muscular tension and bodily symptoms were on one side of the emotional seesaw and crying and verbal expressions, on the other. For as Anthony began to cry more and talk about how he felt, his body relaxed, and his nausea and vomiting were greatly reduced. Furthermore, instead of being depressed for days before and after the injections, he bounced back, maintained a good appetite, and returned to school quickly.

Though crying is the most common way in which children express their fears, it is by no means the only way. The child who must face an uncomfortable medical procedure should be allowed to talk about being afraid, to say it hurts, and to communicate how angry he is. It is not unusual for young children to personalize pain—to equate the sensation of pain with the person who is seen as responsible for causing it. While receiving injections, some youngsters will shout out that they hate the doctor or the nurse. Though most parents strive to teach their children manners, during an injection is not the best time for an etiquette lesson. Often, once the shot is over, the child will seem perfectly unaware of having insulted the health professional and will resume a friendly demeanor. Getting used to being a temporary villain is one of the adjustments that beginning pediatricians and pediatric nurses undergo at the outset of their training. The doctor or nurse with a modicum of experience will not be overly sensitive to such temporary hostility on the part of young patients and will view it as an occupational hazard.

Parents should let a child know that it's all right to cry or shout, but that he must *hold still* and physically cooperate during a procedure so that the injection or examination can be carried out with a minimum of delay or repetition. In situations where the child's crying *directly* interferes with the procedure, such as during dental examinations, he can be offered alternative ways to express his feelings. For example, he can be provided with a ball of clay and told that all the angry or hurt feelings can be squeezed into the clay. Permission to take a favorite toy or plaything with him as he sits in the dental chair—if the toy isn't one that has the potential to obstruct the dentist's work—offers the dual function of providing distraction and an outlet for emotional expression.

Don't assume that when the procedure is over it has passed completely from the youngster's mind. Research has shown that it takes a while for anxious feelings to subside and that the more painful the procedure the longer the time for recuperation can be. Younger children, especially those under six, tend to take the longest to "bounce back." Because of this I recommend that parents provide the child with opportunities to express his feelings. Allow him to talk, do not dismiss him by saying "Oh, that's all over with, you don't have to worry about it" and provide the tools for nonverbal expression. Gentle encouragement to draw pictures of the medical procedure can produce artwork that is surprisingly angry and emotionally intense. Often children will relish tearing up their drawings and throwing them out. In this way, they can "get rid" of the unpleasant experience concretely. Post-procedural expression of feelings is particularly important for the child who must undergo a number of repeated medical procedures. Such youngsters often create entire books of drawings that are fascinating barometers of their emotional reactions.

Desensitizing Fear of Needles

We have discussed the value of preparing children for impending medical procedures by guiding them through doctor play as they carry out the injection or examination upon a doll or other surrogate. Some children, however, have been so frightened by medical experiences that they refuse even to come close to objects such as syringes, needles, swabs, and Band-Aids. For such youngsters, a program of *desensitization* can be helpful.

Desensitization involves *gradual* exposure to the object that causes fear while the child engages in behavior that is incompatible with anxiety (the enemies of anxiety discussed in chapter 3). Basically, the child is rewarded for approaching the feared stimulus in a step-by-step manner, moving at his own pace, so that anxious feelings never have a chance to grow intense.

For young children, who do not have an eating problem, food is an ideal reward. Four-year-old Sharon was treated using a feeding technique.

Sharon had been exposed to a battery of blood tests following an infection at the age of three and a half. This experience had so traumatized her that the sight of a hypodermic syringe caused her to turn pale, tremble, and hide behind her mother's skirts. Since she was scheduled for a medical checkup during which she was to receive a vaccination, her parents were concerned about reducing her anxiety.

Due to the intensity of her learned fear, Sharon could not be prepared through direct exposure to needles. She was able, however, to view a small pencil drawing of a hypodermic syringe without getting anxious. This was selected as the first step on her "ladder of fears."

Sharon was asked to hold the drawing and look at it for several minutes. She ate raisins—a favorite food—while doing so and was additionally rewarded with praise. When she remained calm, she was asked if she wanted to look at a bigger drawing and be rewarded with more raisins. She agreed and was successful in holding the larger piece of artwork. Gradually, she was able to:

Look at and hold a small photograph of a needle
Look at and hold a larger photograph
Stand five feet from a small, needle-less syringe
Hold and examine the syringe
Hold and examine a larger syringe
Hold and examine a large syringe with a needle

Sharon moved at her own pace and was rewarded at each step with raisins and praise. Never did her anxiety manifest itself and never was she pushed or pressured. By the time she reached step 6—in two sessions—she was ready to rehearse the upcoming vaccination on a doll. During the injection, Sharon cried and got angry and insisted upon watching the needle go into her arm. When it was all over, she drew angry pictures and threw them away. She also requested, and was granted, permission to repeat the injection several times on the doll surrogate.

Desensitization should never be attempted by an adult who feels anxiety about the procedure. Nor should it be forced upon an unwilling child. Parents who do not feel comfortable using this technique should obtain help from a behaviorally trained child psychologist.

The success of desensitization depends upon several key points:

Finding the first rung on the child's ladder of fear—the point at which he expresses no anxiety.

Finding the appropriate reward for the child by discussing this with him. In Sharon's case this meant raisins. For other youngsters different types of food, money, playing a game, or expressing anger are good anti-anxiety stimuli.

Rewarding approach behavior step by step, never allowing anxiety to grow strong. At the first signs of distress, the parent should take a step backwards and move slowly. For example, one child may be able to progress from standing five feet away from a needle to actually touching it, while another may have to move more slowly—from five to three to one foot—before exposure.

Desensitization is a learning technique. By replacing fearful associations with masterful ones, the child is helped to experience what frightened him in a new way. Providing a reward for approach behavior helps to combat conditioned patterns of avoidance. Placing desensitization in a teamlike context is constructive, and emphasizing the opportunity to earn rewards is appealing to most youngsters.

Coping
with Hospitalization

Studies conducted two decades ago in England and the United States showed that hospitalization can be traumatic for children and that symptoms of anxiety often persist for weeks after the experience. Furthermore, the intensity of a child's psychological reaction is not necessarily related to the medical seriousness of the procedure or illness that caused him to be hospitalized. Anxiety reactions may occur in the face of major or minor procedures if emotional concerns are not dealt with properly. Moreover, there is evidence that anxiety can affect the quality of a child's medical response to surgery or illness. In one study, the children of mothers who were helped to provide psychological support during hospitalization for tonsillectomy had less fever, shorter recovery time, fewer sleep disturbances, and cried less than youngsters whose parents offered no such support.

Hospitalization must be understood as a psychological as

135

well as a medical event. For this reason, I feel that whenever possible, children should be treated in pediatric hospitals that are designed with the patients' emotional needs in mind. There are general hospitals that have excellent pediatric wards, but a childrens hospital is most likely to offer the variety of special programs (to be discussed below) that aid the child in coping with hospitalization. In addition, most good pediatric surgeons and physicians have medical privileges at pediatric medical centers and may prefer to work in an environment that is especially suited to their young patients. Families residing in or near a large urban center are unlikely to have difficulty in finding a qualified doctor who is a member of the staff at a childrens hospital.

The following are some of the ways that hospitalization can have a negative emotional impact upon children. Remedial measures are included.

Separation and Disruption

Being admitted to the hospital means being separated from parents, brothers and sisters, and other loved ones to whom children have grown attached. The younger the child, the greater the potential for separation anxiety. Young children traditionally react to separation or loss in a three-stage manner. First, they actively protest being abandoned—screaming, kicking, exhibiting tantrum behavior, and, in general, attempting to resist. Then, they exhibit signs of despair, which can include withdrawing and huddling in the corner of the crib or bed, refusing food, not talking. Finally, they accept the reality of being left alone and begin to accommodate to their new surroundings. Such adjustment can mean substituting attachment to members of the hospital staff for the broken parent-child bond. Children who have been hospitalized for prolonged periods of time during which they see their parents infrequently can begin to prefer a favorite nurse to Mom or Dad. Some youngsters below the age of three have failed to recognize parents after several weeks of separation. This has been attributed to an intense anger reaction on the part of the small child.

It is also important to understand what separation from the environment means. During hospitalization, the child is removed from his comforting environment, and his normal, day-to-day *routine* is interrupted. I cannot overemphasize the importance of schedules and routines in terms of establishing emotional stability for children. Children get used to waking up at certain times and having their meals during specific periods. They take comfort in familiarity. Daily, repeated patterns of work, play, and social interaction are crucial in developing the child's sense of identity.

The best way to reduce the risk of separation anxiety is to minimize or prevent the separation process itself. Many childrens hospitals have instituted *rooming-in* policies, in which parents or significant adults are allowed to spend the night with the pediatric patient. This is certainly an enlightened attitude, though it is one that met with some initial resistance from hospital administrators and others who found major change difficult. Parents may need to inquire about the existence of rooming-in, or the policy may be openly advertised by the hospital. Faced with a choice of two hospitals that are medically equivalent, I would definitely opt to have my child treated at the one that offered rooming-in. The young child will almost always prefer his parents' presence. Children above the age of eight or nine may choose to forego rooming-in because they have a growing need for independence. In any event ask the child and respect his wishes.

A second approach aimed at reducing the child's stay in

the hospital is the use of *short-admission surgery*. Children undergoing many types of minor surgical procedures do not need to be in the hospital for extended periods of time. Often they can go home the day after the operation, and sometimes, if surgery is performed early in the morning and the patient responds well, there is no need for an overnight stay. Short-admission surgery requires that parents be educated in taking care of their child at home while he recuperates. It also implies recognition of something that most of us have known intuitively for quite some time: *Well-adjusted parents are better equipped to care for their children emotionally than the best trained professionals.* An added benefit of short-admission surgery is a reduced financial burden upon the family, and today, when a night in the hospital can cost more than two hundred dollars, this is a major factor to consider. Once again, it may be necessary for parents to take the initiative in discussing with the surgeon whether or not short-admission surgery is appropriate for the proposed operation, and if the hospital offers it.

Many pediatric hospitals have also relaxed their rules about sibling visits. In recent years health professionals have come to appreciate the importance of viewing the family as a unit and understanding that hospitalization or any other event that disrupts the family-life pattern affects each and every family member. Restricting a young patient's brothers and sisters from visiting him because they fall below some arbitrary minimum age level is psychologically insensitive. Siblings need to understand what is going on with the hospitalized child. Otherwise they run the risk of developing anxiety-provoking fantasies.

For example, it is quite common for brothers and sisters to develop *contagion fears*—worries about "catching" whatever it is that the hospitalized child has. Youngsters hear so much about staying away from those who are sick that it is not surprising that contagion anxiety develops even when no communicable disease is present.

Another potentially harmful fantasy involves *survivor guilt*. The healthy child may wonder why his sibling is in the hospital while he has been spared such a fate. The guilt that can develop from such thoughts can lead to anxiety and self-punishment such as loss of appetite and sleep, and in rare cases, psychosomatic mimicking of the ill child's symptoms.

Sibling jealousy can develop when the healthy brother or sister sees the hospitalized child receiving special attention, gifts, or privileges. Though parental rooming-in is helpful for the patient in the hospital, care must be taken that children at home are not neglected.

The best way to deal with sibling concerns is to make sure that brothers and sisters fully understand why a sibling is going to the hospital and to have them participate in the process. Efforts should be made to include every member of the family in the hospitalization experience. This means encouraging questions and discussion on the part of all children and allowing for open expression of feelings, as well as regular visits. Some particularly progressive hospitals have begun to offer *drop-in centers* for siblings of pediatric patients. These are places where brothers and sisters can learn about medical aspects of various diseases and surgical procedures, engage in therapeutic play, and become comfortable with the hospital environment. Including siblings in the hospitalization process helps minimize separation anxiety both for them and for the patient. It also is a first step in preventing disruption of family schedules and routines.

There are additional measures that aid in maintaining the hospitalized child's psychological equilibrium. First, as in the case of doctor visits, it helps to prepare children for the fact that they are going into the hospital. Adequate time should be provided for the youngster to understand the medical reasons for his admission as well as for him to ask pertinent questions and receive truthful answers. More will be said about this in the section on Fear of the Unknown.

In order to establish continuity between the home and hospital environment, children should be permitted to bring one or more favorite toys or objects with them. Such transitional objects—''security blankets''—should be of the patient's choosing and may be toys, dolls, articles of clothing, favorite books, or pictures. They serve to remind the child of home in a tangible manner and reaffirm his identity as a *child who happens to be in the hospital* rather than as a *patient*.

When it appears that hospitalization is going to last for more than a few days, active efforts should be made to maintain the child's school participation. Many youngsters have spoken to me about how frightening it is to return to school after an absence as short as one week. After only a few days in a new and often frightening environment, anxiety begins to build up about what the world outside is like. In addition, falling behind in school can make the return to class difficult, particularly for the child who is concerned about academic performance and sets high standards for himself. Obtaining copies of class material that will be studied during the period of hospitalization is often quite simple if teachers are approached beforehand. Some school districts have mandated that youngsters who remain in the hospital for more than a minimum number of days be provided the services of a *hospital schoolteacher* whose job it is to coordinate special education programs for pediatric patients. These educational specialists often work out of the major childrens hospital in the community and provide invaluable service in preserving scholastic continuity.

During lengthy hospital stays, maintenance of prior schedules and routines becomes especially important. Parents can work with the nursing staff to duplicate, as closely as possible, the waking times, mealtimes, and bedtimes that the child was accustomed to at home. Obviously, there will be instances when this will not be feasible. But parents who let the hospital staff know that adherence to familiar routines is a concern can maximize the probability that some sense of stability will be attained. Children who can tell time should be provided with access to a clock or watch. This helps orient them and reduces the "jarring" experience that many children have described, in which there is heightened confusion about time and space when they return home.

Though parental rooming-in can reduce the trauma of separation, there will be many times when parental absence is unavoidable. In such cases, firm schedules of visitation and telephone calls should be set up *and adhered to*. There are few things sadder than the expression on a young patient's face when the phone call that was supposed to come at four o'clock doesn't materialize. Don't promise more visits or contacts than are possible and avoid vague commitments to "come to see you soon." Specific times of day should be established. For the youngster who cannot tell time, diagrams using the face of a clock can be utilized or associations can be made to familiar activities. The nursing staff should be informed of the visitation and call schedule so that they can answer the child's questions accurately.

It is also helpful if parents take turns visiting the hospitalized child. In this way Mother and Father become equally involved in the experience and all children in the family have access to both of them. This also helps in promoting good communication between parents. It is not unusual for fathers to become resentful when their wives seem to be spending every waking minute at the hospital. Though such feelings of jealousy may seem selfish or petty, they are natural. By undertaking "hospital duty," Dad can better understand his child's health as well as his wife's behavior. In other words, *balanced participation* leads to increased empathy and family unity.

Pain and Discomfort

Almost any hospitalization will involve some degree of pain for the young patient. This may come in the form of frequent blood tests, probes, scans, or injections. The techniques of preparatory doll play (surrogate play) and desensitization discussed in chapter 7 (Going to the Doctor and the Dentist) are especially useful in the hospital. In many pediatric medical centers, there are trained professionals whose job it is to offer such services under programs such as *Patient Activity* or *Child Life*. These specialists usually have a master's degree in child development, special education, nursing, or equivalent training. Child Life programs are less common in general hospitals and are another reason why it is best for children to be treated in medical facilities that are designed especially for them.

Most Child Life or Patient Activity specialists use as home-bases *hospital playrooms* situated directly on the wards. In these havens, children are assisted in learning about their disease and/or surgeries, prepared for procedures, and given the opportunity to express their feelings about what is happening to their bodies. A peek into a typical hospital playroom may reveal a group of children busy with doctor play while several other youngsters compile hospital diaries. Still another gathering may be engaged in body tracings that help define the child's physical and psychological self-image. In addition to these therapeutic activities, hospital playrooms provide recreational activities for patients that help reduce the tedium and boredom of a hospital stay. By promoting contact with other children who are undergoing similar experiences, such activities help minimize the child's sense of isolation and of being different from his peers. This type of stimulation is especially important for the patient who is unlikely to be receiving numerous visitors. Parents should inquire if the hospital has a Patient Activity program and if the ward where their child is to be staying has access to a playroom. In the case of a lengthy hospitalization combined with substantial separation, early contact should be established with the Patient Activity specialist so that special care will be taken regarding the youngster's emotional needs.

In addition to techniques such as surrogate doll play, some hospitals make use of educational motion pictures or videotapes that illustrate, in detail, specific medical and surgical procedures. For example, a child about to undergo a tonsillectomy may be shown a short film in which he views another child going through this experience. This makes use of the principle of therapeutic modeling in an especially creative way. The patient identifies with the child on the screen and learns to imitate responses that are productive and adaptive. At the same time, he observes the role model go through the surgical experience and come out of it successfully. This reduces fear and builds greater confidence and hope. There is considerable evidence that a healthy attitude promotes more rapid healing and recuperation. To the extent that psychological methods of preparation promote ''positive thinking,'' they serve to directly enhance the child's physical response to illness and surgery.

Some physicians prefer to use sedation while administering medical procedures, such as spinal taps and isotopic scans, to children. This is done both out of genuine concern for the child's welfare and because of the doctor's wish to get the procedure over as quietly and quickly as possible. I do not feel that sedation is appropriate in most cases. Many children have reported to me, and to my colleagues, that though they *appeared* calm while being tranquilized, the drugs brought about a heightened (and invisible) sense of helplessness and anxiety. Children have even said that they felt more pain under sedation than without chemical assistance. In support of this, it should be noted that the American Medical Association has come out against the use of tranquilization or sedation for minor pediatric procedures. My experience has been that the vast majority of children who have been adequately prepared for tests, pokes, sticks, and probes do not profit from sedation. Of course, there will be certain highly anxious children who become hysterical unless a tranquilizing drug is administered. In such instances, appropriate medication must be used, but this should be followed up with psychological therapy.

Needless to say, hospitalized children should never be admonished not to cry or express their feelings. Neither should they be expected to be "good" patients—perfectly compliant, passive, quiet, and unquestioning—in the face of physical and psychological assault. Given the opportunity to experience some degree of mastery and control within the medical setting, youngsters can go through one or several hospitalizations without incurring permanent or serious psychological damage.

Fear of the Unknown

A child's mind abhors a vacuum. In the absence of accurate information, fantasies that are often worse than reality take over. For this reason, a policy of trying to hide things from a young patient, besides being harmful, is impossible. Professionals who have worked in medical settings know that there are few secrets kept in hospitals. Children hear their "case" being discussed by interns, residents, nurses, attending physicians, their own parents, perhaps, and other patients and their parents. Often, because of these bits and pieces of conversation, the child constructs a highly distorted picture of why he is in the hospital. Such unreal and potentially frightening fantasies are strengthened by inaccurate explanations given by parents and other well-meaning adults. The case of Davey illustrates this.

Davey, a previously well-adjusted five-year-old boy, was referred for psychological consultation several weeks after his release from the hospital for treatment of a viral infection. Since his return home, his parents reported that he had grown increasingly "clingy" and refused to separate from them even for brief periods of time. His appetite dropped, and he slept fitfully. A physical examination revealed no organic cause for these symptoms.

During play therapy, Davey drew pictures of himself in the hospital. Each drawing contained a small figure of a boy whose body was filled with dozens of many-legged creatures. When asked what these were, he replied:

"This is a sick boy with bugs inside of him. They are eating him up."

Subsequent discussion with Davey's mother revealed that he had asked her why he was in the hospital and that she had told him:

"Oh, it's nothing. You just have a bug inside you and the doctors are trying to get rid of it."

To an adult, "having a bug" is clearly a colloquial expression, and the mature mind quickly interprets and makes sense out of such a statement. A five-year-old's tendency to take things literally—to deal in concrete terms—transforms such a casual statement into a terrifying fantasy. After Davey understood that viruses were not bugs but tiny "dots" that did not eat little children and were killed by medicine, his anxious symptoms disappeared.

Incomplete or inaccurate understanding of disease processes is not unique to small children. One of my research colleagues, a professor of adolescent medicine, regularly collects drawings by teen-age patients, and these usually reveal a considerable amount of distorted thinking. In fact, many adults who are ill or hospitalized do not fully understand what is happening to them. But the younger the person is, the more likely such fantasies are to create disturbances.

Age and development affect the way children view illness causality. If you pose the question "Why do people get sick?" to a group of preschoolers, most responses will be generalized, inaccurate, and circular ("You get sick by kissing bald people" or "Taking weird pills makes you sick" or "You get sick when you feel bad"). Children between the ages of six and nine begin to understand some connection between physical events and illness, but these tend to be limited, mechanical, and extremely concrete ("Sickness is started when peanuts go down the wrong tube in your mouth" or "When you cut your finger you become sick"). Most youngsters above nine years of age have the ability to understand illness causality in terms of abstract concepts ("You catch diseases from germs carried by other people").

These age ranges are approximate and only apply to children with little or no medical experience. The child who, for one reason or another, goes through hospitalization several times may become knowledgeable and sophisticated beyond his years. I have known three-year-olds who include in their vocabulary such words as "sterilize," "injection," "intravenous," and "therapy" and use these terms accurately.

Youngsters in the six-to-nine-year range make especially strong connections between breaking rules and becoming ill. They may develop guilt reactions about being sick. I have encountered many children with different types of acute or chronic illnesses who were certain that their problem came about because they misbehaved or didn't listen to their parents or forgot to put on a sweater. The guilt-ridden child operates under a double burden. He must cope with the pain and suffering of illness as well as the anguish of believing that he has brought it all upon himself. In order to minimize this, children should always be presented with medically accurate explanations for why they are being treated or having an operation.

Physicians should play a large role in this type of explanation. The child regards his doctor as someone very powerful and is likely to put great stock in what he is told by the man or woman in white. Many physicians are conscientious about communicating accurately and age-appropriately to their young patients. Unfortunately, this is not always the case. One prominent and highly skilled pediatric surgeon told me that he seldom talks to most of the children upon whom he operates. Residents observe the child before surgery, the anesthesiologist conducts an examination that involves more reading of the medical chart than it does face-to-face discussion. When conversation does take place, it is often between doctor and parent. The child, the star of the show, is often shunted to the sidelines. The first time the surgeon sees the patient is in the operating room, just prior to the administration of anesthesia. Parents may need to ask their doctor for explanations for their own understanding as well as to make sure that the child has an accurate idea about what is going on.

Some pediatric hospitals provide written booklets and brochures about diseases and medical procedures that are geared both for parents and for children of various ages. Children's material may include coloring books that help the child actively participate in psychologically mastering disease-related information. Youngsters should be encouraged to make use of such materials.

One specific fear that some children develop involves the connection they make between anesthesia ("being put to sleep") and death. Youngsters may be afraid of not waking up and may find it difficult to understand how a knife cutting through their skin will not hurt if they are alive. This happens when the child has previously learned to associate sleep and death: when someone dies he "goes to sleep for a long, long time" or an animal is "put to sleep" or "put out of its misery." It is vital that sleep and death not be associated in the child's mind and that they be presented as two very different things. More will be said about this in chapter 13 (A Death in the Family). Anesthesia can be presented as a type of sleep during which the child may or may not have dreams, but from which he will *always* wake up. Children need also to be reassured that the doctor will make sure that they will not wake up until the operation is over and that the doctor will take good care of them. It is best for a youngster to hear this from both the anesthesiologist and his parents.

There is no fear greater than the fear of the unknown. Parents are so concerned with protecting their children from harm that they may tend to forget this and attempt to shield youngsters from reality. Besides the fact that this leads to fantasies that can be more frightening than the truth, a special burden is placed on the child. He knows that it is not okay to talk about being sick or being in the hospital, because his attempts to discuss these topics have been put off with answers such as "Oh, it's nothing" or "Don't worry about it, I'll take care of it" or "You're too young to understand." In addition to going through separation fears, pain, discomfort, and life disruption, he cannot even communicate his feelings to those in whom he places his trust. This leads to feelings of isolation and helplessness. The true test of good parent-child communication occurs when issues of genuine concern and serious emotional content arise for discussion. Rather than sheltering children, it is better to arm them with understanding and guide them in gaining some degree of mastery over experiences such as hospitalization and illness.

Regression

Becoming a patient in a hospital means giving up a great deal of control.

The newly admitted patient—child or adult—trades his clothing for a uniform that resembles, more than slightly, an infant's nightgown. He stops walking and lies down. He is expected to stay in bed and allow others to take care of his basic needs. His identity is reduced to a bracelet around the wrist and a manila chart that he is not allowed to look at. Meals are brought to him. He may even be required to urinate and defecate in a passive manner, using a bedpan, and to have his excrement collected. To a certain extent, being a "good" patient means acting in a compliant, dependent manner. When this pattern of enforced passivity is combined with anxiety, it is not hard to see why some hospitalized patients begin to show signs of regression—behaving in a manner that is appropriate for someone younger.

Regression may take the form of bedwetting in a child who was previously toilet trained, or of a youngster's reluctance to do things for himself. Usually it is not a serious or long-standing problem, but one that represents a temporary reaction to a new environment. There are steps that can be taken to minimize the chance of regressive behavior.

Children in the hospital should be encouraged to do things for themselves as much as is medically appropriate. By taking an active role in his own care, the young patient is less likely to grow dependent or feel helpless. When the doctor prescribes bed rest, this must be adhered to. However, more than one might imagine, it is feasible for the recuperating child to feed himself and engage in moderate exercise such as walking around. When hospital playrooms are provided, children should be encouraged to get up out of bed and make use of them. Unless the hospital has stiff regulations about wearing uniforms, it is best to let the child dress in his normal, everyday street clothes. Most childrens' hospitals, have, in fact, begun to encourage this. The basic idea behind this is to promote the continuation of as much of the child's previous behavior patterns as possible, in order to establish *continuity*. The more normal we keep the environment, the more likely we are to promote normal behavior.

One issue that is often overlooked in hospitals is *privacy*. Many children who enter the hospital with strongly developed attitudes about privacy find it a struggle to maintain psychological integrity in the face of frequent examinations and procedures that may take place in front of many spectators. The very process of medical rounds, during which senior physicians instruct interns, residents, and medical students at the patient's bedside can cause considerable invasion of privacy. Rounds originated during the days when most of what was to be known about medicine came from visually examining the patient's body. Today, although most clinical teaching involves a review of the medical chart and there may be little need to actually observe the patient, the process continues, as something of a ritual. Unfortunately, rounds are sometimes accompanied by a discussion of the youngster that is conducted as if he did not exist. Young patients, especially adolescents, grow resentful of having their "case" discussed within earshot with no attempt made to involve them or acknowledge their presence. Adults should understand that an eight-year-old likes no better than they would to be considered "the adenoidectomy in Room 302." Strenous efforts should be made to honor the young patient's sense of identity and self-worth.

In the event that regressive behavior does arise, and this may take the form of increased clinginess and passivity, bedwetting, and speech and appetite problems, it is best not to make a fuss about it. Once the child has returned home and settled into familiar routines, such symptoms usually disappear. Regression that lasts for more than a few weeks should be handled through professional consultation.

Going Home

The impact of hospitalization does not end when the child walks out through the hospital exit. It is unrealistic to expect all youngsters to "pigeon-hole" their feelings and snap back to the way they were just because they are, physically, back home. Some children do adjust immediately, while others take a few days. Occasionally children may complain of feeling confused or disoriented after hospitalization. This occurs when the child has been in an especially quiet, nonstimulating hospital ward and finds the sudden return to the busy outside world an extreme perceptual contrast. Confusion is often expressed by such comments as "Everything seems so noisy" or "The car is going so fast!" Such disorientation is normal, temporary, and no cause for alarm. It will subside if no fuss is made about it.

The basic thing to remember in helping the child return as quickly as possible to his prehospitalization behavior, is to *avoid giving him special treatment.* Just as is the case with chronically ill children, it is tempting to overprotect the recently hospitalized child and relax standards of discipline. This serves to let the child know that he is viewed as incompetent, weak, ill, and *different.* If a youngster was expected to keep his room clean before his appendectomy, and his doctor says that he is physically capable of resuming this, he should not be allowed to avoid responsibility. The same goes for school. Return the child as quickly as possible to class and do not allow habitual patterns of avoidance to grow. Children benefit from learning that life goes on despite occasional stress and that their parents have confidence in their ability to handle things. Parents who continue to maintain normal standards of discipline, structure, and responsibility help build the child's sense of self-worth. By viewing himself as competent, the child can learn to regard his experience in the hospital as one that he handled *successfully*. In this way, something positive is distilled from an otherwise stressful experience.

Changing Hospital Policy

We have discussed several approaches that aid the child in coping with hospitalization—rooming-in, liberal visitation policies, sibling drop-in centers, Patient Activity programs, hospital playrooms, hospital schoolteachers, and educational motion pictures. While many childrens' hospitals make use of one or all of these, there are many medical facilities that do not. Why is this so, if research and clinical experience reveal their usefulness time and time again?

The answer is that hospitals—private or public—are *businesses*. They are run by administrators whose primary interest is in keeping the account books balanced. Though several studies have shown that psychological support programs lead to decreased hospital costs—because well-adjusted patients make fewer visits and recuperate faster—such cost effectiveness is hard to prove for an individual institution. Since special programs do not directly bring in revenue, administrators are sometimes reluctant to spend the money to implement them.

On the other hand, as businessmen, administrators are particularly sensitive to consumer opinion. Without patients, hospitals would not last very long. This gives parents and children more power than they might have thought they had. Letters to administrators that specify which aspects of the child's hospitalization were positive and which were not are potent agents for change. The administrator who receives several letters commending the hospital for its excellent playroom and preparation techniques is going to develop increased enthusiasm for these programs. Similarly, consistent patterns of complaints about the lack of emotional support for patients will lead to at least some degree of head-scratching and re-calculating. The point is, a hospital exists to serve the physical and emotional needs of the patient. As guardians of childrens' welfare, parents have considerable power and the right to assert themselves in pressing for health care programs that meet these needs.

Common
Childhood Fears

Children—and adults—can learn to be afraid of almost anything. There are, however, certain objects or events that tend commonly to elicit fearful reactions. Here are some of them:

Animals

Some psychologists and psychiatrists view childhood fears as symptoms of deep, underlying psychological problems. According to this point of view, the feared object is not the *cause* of anxiety but merely a *symbol* of something else that is subconsciously frightening. Therapists who practice Freudian psychoanalysis are likely to see animals as sexual symbols and fear of animals as evidence of sexual conflict. In fact, one of Freud's earliest published cases involved a young boy who was afraid of horses. According to Freud's interpretation, horses symbolized the boy's father, and his fear was not directly related to animals at all.

At the opposite end of the spectrum are those doctors who see fear of animals—and other childhood anxiety reactions—in a more straightforward manner. They believe that there is little scientific evidence to support the notion that specific childhood fears grow out of deeply buried psychological problems. On the contrary, most fearful youngsters are otherwise well-adjusted.

In addition, there is no scientific evidence that lengthy psychoanalysis aimed at uncovering the subconscious conflicts is effective in combatting children's fears. In fact, some psychoanalysts have come around to the point of view that it is necessary to deal directly with fear as a learned set of behaviors. There are literally hundreds of successful case histories and research studies in which a direct approach to un-learning fear has proved rapidly successful. In the vast majority of these, no "symptom substitution" took place. (Symptom substitution refers to the replacement of one problem with another. According to Freudian theory, this will occur when a deep, underlying conflict is not dealt with.)

Though animals are commonly viewed as symbolic according to the more analytic schools of psychological thought (dogs may be seen as symbols of castration, cats as representing feminine attributes, snakes as phalluses, etc.), my own point of view is that if a child is afraid of dogs, he is afraid of dogs. Period. This is not to say that fears of animals develop in isolation. Parental modeling is important, as in the level of stress in the home. However, in order to help the child with anxiety related to animals, I advocate a direct approach, unhindered by speculation.

There will be times when fear of various animals develops as the result of an actual face-to-face trauma. The child who is bitten by a dog can, understandably, quickly learn negative associations to canine creatures. He may generalize his fears so that various attributes of dogs—barks, tails, flea collars—cause him to feel uncomfortable.

In other instances indirect exposure to stressful, animal-related information may cause fear to develop. A child may watch a friend being attacked, or he may view material on television or in the movies that is anxiety-provoking. A good example of the latter is the movie *Jaws*, which caused increased shark-fear in many adults and children who never actually came into contact with sharks.

In helping the child with animal fears, make use of the following principles:

Encourage Gradual Exposure. Don't force the fearful child to confront the large, snarling dog that terrified him. Such rites of passage serve only to increase his sense of helplessness. Rather, find something related to dogs that is not fear provoking. This may be a young puppy, a photograph, or a cartoon of a dog.

Use Participant Modeling and Rewards for Approach Behavior. Let the child watch as you handle the puppy or picture. Gently guide—but don't force—him to pet the dog along with you and offer praise that emphasizes both the dog's positive qualities and the child's ability to be in control. ("Oh, isn't this little puppy cute. He's so soft." "You really know how to handle him." "I'm proud of you.")

Parents can unwittingly *cue* fearful reactions in an already frightened child. Knowing that seven-year-old Billy is anxious about cats, his father tenses up, ever so slightly, as the two of them approach a wandering feline. This gives Billy the signal that it is time to be afraid. What is happening here is that the father's own anxiety about his son's fear causes him to become an accomplice in the negative learning pattern. On the other hand, if Billy's father casually approaches the cat, making no big fuss one way or another, the boy has the opportunity to observe adaptive behavior and learn from it.

In cases where fear of a particular animal or set of animals is longstanding, it will be helpful to use concrete rewards for approach behavior. A four-year-old child who is afraid of dogs can be encouraged to approach a puppy while enjoying a few bites of a favorite food. Since food is incompatible with anxiety in young children, this helps get rid of fearful associations.* Older children may prefer small amounts of money or earning a privilege.

Systematic Progress and Record Keeping. Once the child is totally comfortable approaching the initial stimulus, be it a puppy, kitten, or picture, he should be gently encouraged to come into contact with something a bit more anxiety provoking. This can be an especially docile cat or small dog. First, a parent or trusted adult should model approaching the new stimulus and then the child should be given the opportunity to touch and hold the animal. Once again, rewards should be offered in the form of praise or more tangible incentives when necessary.

Encourage the child to keep written records of his progress. An ordinary calendar may be used, or parent and child can work together constructing a special chart. The child should record successful attainment of a goal. For example, the fear "chart" of one child looked something like this:

Sarah's Progress

1. Small puppy, ten feet away.   Sunday, I PM
2. Small puppy, touch briefly.   Sunday, 1:15 PM
3. Small puppy, hold for two minutes   Sunday, 1:40 PM
4. Small puppy, hold for ten minutes   Monday, 12:00 NOON
5. Small dog, touch   Monday, 12:30 PM

* Care should be taken not to excessively or exclusively use edible rewards, as a preoccupation with oral gratification can lead to obesity.

6. Small dog, pet for two minutes   Monday, 12:40 PM
7. Small dog, pet for ten minutes   Monday, 1:00 PM
8. Small dog, hold for two minutes   Monday, 1:30 PM

Total

This youngster was able to go through the eight steps in two days. She charted her progress, which emphasized her success, and received a point for the completion of each step. The eight points were redeemed for a trip to the movies with her parents.

Set Realistic Goals. It is not necessary that all children love all animals or that a particular child become totally fearless in the presence of animals. In fact, such lofty goals can be harmful in that they reduce the probability of success. In addition, there will be times when fear of a genuinely dangerous animal is an important protective response. Children should be taught to "read" animal body language. Bared teeth and raised short hairs communicate something quite different from the message conveyed by a wagging tail. Youngsters can readily learn how to interpret such signals and judge an animal's probable behavior.

Having pets can be an instructive, as well as enjoyable, experience, as it helps promote a sense of responsibility and caring. Some children may not care to have pets, while others will crave a home menagerie. This will of course, depend upon parental attitudes. Given his parents' permission, however, the child should be able to make a real choice and not be limited in his life experiencs because of fear.

The Dark

The fertile imaginations of young children enable them to "see" frightening things after the lights have been shut off.

Young children are especially vulnerable to confusing mental imagery with reality. They may become absolutely convinced that goblins and monsters lurk in the shadows of their bedroom.

Some youngsters associate darkness with being left alone or being lost. They may also report feeling dizzy or perceptually confused. This can occur because the pathways of visual perception are cut off in the dark and it is easy to lose one's frame of reference regarding space, depth, and perspective.

Still other children have learned to associate darkness with death. This may result from inaccurate explanations about death in which darkness is emphasized. In these youngsters, fear of the dark is actually a manifestation of death anxiety. More will be said about this in chapter 13 (A Death in the Family).

The gradual-exposure approach combined with reward for success can be used effectively in cases of fear of the dark. The first step is to allow the child to talk about what is bothering him and offer gentle reassurance and explanations. For instance, in the case of the child who associates darkness with death, he should be taught the difference between the two and offered a positive description of darkness—one that emphasizes darkness as a comforting state that allows us to rest and fall asleep more easily.

For the child with persistent fear of the dark, I favor the use of a night light accompanied by *gradual systematic reduction in wattage*. The first week the child and parent might agree that the goal is to sleep with a 20 watt bulb. Accomplishing this will constitute success and each successful night should be rewarded. The next week, a 15 or 10 watt bulb might be substituted, and after that a mini-bulb with a minute amount of illumination can be used. Finally, the child can learn to feel comfortable in the dark room if a night light is left shining in a nearby bathroom.

The child who is afraid of the dark should also be offered a menu of counter-anxious behaviors such as listening to his radio when he starts to feel afraid or thinking of going to a favorite place. He can be allowed to switch on the light for *short* periods when he is anxious, but should be encouraged to eventually restore the room to a state of darkness or semi-darkness.

Parental behavior will have a major influence upon how the child copes with the darkness. The following case illustrates this.

Andrea, a nine-year-old girl, was referred to me because she grew extremely upset when placed in her room with the lights out. Consequently, the light was left on at night, and this hindered her from falling asleep. In desperation, Andrea's parents had begun to take her into their bed at night, although they knew this was not advisable.

This girl's fears could be traced to a camping trip a year earlier, during which she had been left alone in a trailer, surrounded by strange forest noises. After a half hour of solitude, she was in a state of near hysteria.

Two additional factors contributed to Andrea's fear. Her neighborhood had been plagued by several episodes of nocturnal crime—burglaries and auto thefts—that made her feel even more anxious about being left alone in the dark. On top of this, her father had reported—perhaps confessed is more accurate—that he, too, found it difficult to sleep without a night light and that he had been this way since childhood. (Interestingly, Andrea was an adopted child so that the similarity between her and her father's anxiety could not be traced to genetics. This was clearly a learned pattern and one in which parental modeling was far from subtle!)

Andrea spoke of being afraid of robbers and, at my request, she drew a picture of a robber. This turned out to be a skulking figure holding a large sack while standing in the corner of her bedroom. I asked her why he had the sack, and she said that the robber put children in it. Then she told me that the person in the drawing was not really a burglar at all. He was a kidnapper.

First we made sure that Andrea's house was really safe and secure. After this was verified, we used anger as an enemy of anxiety. Andrea drew pictures of the kidnapper, got mad at him, tore up the drawings, and threw them away. She was encouraged to get mad any time she started to feel afraid. She agreed to start sleeping in her room with a 25 watt bulb in the lamp near her bed. She was rewarded for appropriate sleep with points that could be redeemed for an outing with her parents. The following week the wattage in the bulb was reduced to 15. This systematic reduction continued until she was able to sleep comfortably in the dark. Simultaneously, her father took the initiative to try a similar process for himself. Not wanting to be out-done by his daughter, he was rapidly successful in combatting his own anxiety.

As is true of children with insomnia and nightmares, special care should be taken that the youngster with fear of the dark is relaxed at bedtime. Parental reassurance and comfort accompanied by a brief period of pleasurable activities before lights out are valuable. The child should not be allowed to postpone bedtime because of his fears and if an impasse is reached, it is preferable to allow a night light to remain shining rather than engage in a lengthy power struggle.

Water

Children who have experienced loss of control while swimming or in the bath may develop anxiety about being placed in water. Being swept under by a big wave, or being "dunked" for an extended period are the types of events that can trigger such fears.

Anxious youngsters should not be thrown into the pool in an attempt to quickly "cure" their fears. It is a myth that such sink-or-swim tactics are effective. More commonly they serve to increase the youngster's terror. As with most fearful reactions, a gradual approach works best and imposes minimal stress upon parent and child.

It is valuable for children to be taught how to swim at an early age so that they feel relaxed and in control in an aquatic environment. This becomes especially important if the family home is equipped with a pool. Many two-and-a-half or three-year-old children find learning to swim very easy and enjoyable. In some communities, aquatic classes are offered for children as young as three months. While there is no harm in exposing healthy infants to water, and many babies seem to enjoy splashing in the pool with Mommy and Daddy, it is unrealistic to expect that this training will carry over to later comfort in the water. Human babies naturally make swimming movements at an early age, but they lose this ability—there is no generalization from infancy to toddler stages as far as water skills are concerned. The practice of holding babies' heads under water in order for them to get accustomed to holding their breath should be discouraged. Most infants choke, sputter, and gain nothing from the experience other than several seconds of discomfort.

I recall seeing a set of underwater photographs taken of a four-month-old who had been given "swimming" lessons during which his head was held under water. The swimming instructor was sure that the little boy enjoyed this and assured the parents that this would toughen him up for future aquatic training. The photographs revealed something quite contrary to this, however. The look on the little boy's face was one of abject terror—there was not a trace of enjoyment. Not surprisingly, this baby became anxious the next time he was brought to the pool. His parents discontinued the lessons and resumed them when he was two years old. At this age he enjoyed mastering how to swim (at another swim school).

Water fears are almost always short-lived. The child who persists in his anxiety can be helped through participant modeling—having a trusted adult guide him gradually into the water, as he experiences feelings of fun, relaxation, and mastery. Increased pressure to perform will only raise the level of anxiety.

Body Changes

At about the age of eight or nine, many children become preoccupied with their bodies. There can be temporary stages of bodily worries that appear almost hypochondriacal in nature, with the child frequently complaining of feeling ill or strange or asking anxious questions about his health. During this phase, children may also avoid certain foods for fear of getting sick or "being poisoned." Such worries are usually transitory, although in families where issues of health and illness are overemphasized, there is increased chance that children will develop chronic anxiety about their bodies. The best way to handle this type of anxiety is to offer reassurance and comfort without making a big fuss. Parents can emphasize the assertive, masterful, and competent things that children do and give praise for these so that it becomes clear that well-being is the prized attribute in the family, not illness. In addition, parents who experienced similar anxieties when they were children can help by communicating this and making it clear that such fears pass.

Occasionally, distorted body-image is the result of confusing information given to the young or especially impressionable child. Dr. Michael Wayne of Provincial General Hospital in Alberta, Canada, reported the case of a five-year-old girl who was taught the following lesson in Sunday school:

Read your Bible, pray every day, and you will grow, grow, grow;

Neglect your Bible and refuse to pray, and you will shrink, shrink, shrink.

In addition to learning this lesson, Dr. Wayne's patient read a comic book in which "shrinking men" were the main characters. Not surprisingly, this little girl developed an anxiety reaction in which she was convinced her hand was shrinking. Dr. Wayne's treatment involved having her trace her hand on a piece of cardboard. Then, each time she spoke of shrinking hands, she was asked to hold her hand up against the tracing so that she could, concretely, see that no change in size had occurred. Combined with this, the little girl's parents were instructed to stop giving her undue attention in response to her anxious statements but to be matter-of-fact and use the cardboard. They were also told to look out for appropriate play behaviors and praise these. Finally, the child was transferred to another Sunday school. Within eleven days the fear of shrinkage was gone.

Concerns about body changes become especially important during puberty. Actual hormonal changes affect how the adolescent feels about himself. For example, there is evidence that testosterone, the male sex hormone, promotes feelings of aggressiveness and activity. It is the rare teen-ager who is totally content with the various changes that his body is going through. Boys may find their voices too high and squeaky or too gruff and low or may discover, to their horror, that their vocal chords give out and "crack" at embarrassing moments. Girls who develop breasts at an early age often become self-conscious, while their peers who remain "flat-chested" a bit longer worry about being unfeminine. Skin blemishes are, of course, the scourge of a high proportion of preadolescents and adolescents. Development of secondary sexual characteristics can be anxiety provoking both in terms of pace—occurring too soon or not soon enough—and the accompanying sexual feelings that go with this bodily change. Girls unprepared for the onset of menstruation can be traumatized during an initial bleeding episode.

There is very little that parents can do in terms of directly changing the rate of pubescent change. Each adolescent's body will metamorphose at its own rate. Parents can, however, affect the *quality* of adjustment that their teen-age sons and daughters experience by offering support and comfort and by sharing some of their own experiences as teen-agers. Such self-disclosure serves several purposes. It lets the teen-ager know that the things that are happening to his body are not unusual or abnormal, thus reducing his sense of isolation and fear of the unknown. It helps prepare him for future change and opens up channels of communication. In addition, hearing Mom or Dad talk about their own skin problems or their worries over breast development and beard growth and finding out that such concerns were dealt with successfully promotes optimism and hope. Even though many adolescents rebel against parental authority and may not appear to place much value on the judgment of their elders, they continue to look up to their mothers and fathers. Only when extreme and longstanding hostility exists between parent and child does this cease.

It is probably best for adolescents to discuss issues of physical change with the same-sex parent, for this makes the parental experience more applicable. Also, since many patterns of physiological growth are genetic, there are likely to be similarities between the rate at which fathers and sons and mothers and daughters develop. The father who observes his son's concern over not developing beard growth as rapidly as his peers and who went through the same process is in an excellent position to provide empathy and support. Similarly, mothers are uniquely able to communicate with their daughters regarding the experience of menstruation. When both parents are not living in the home or same-sex parent-child communication is not feasible for some other reason, the parent of the opposite sex who is nonjudgmental and willing to listen and share personal experiences can be extremely therapeutic for his or her adolescent.

Separation

We have discussed separation anxiety in several contexts in previous chapters under sleep disorders, school avoidance, and hospitalization. The theme of separation fears will occur and recur in any discussion that attempts comprehensively to cover anxiety in children, because fear of abandonment is a focal concern of most children under six or seven. Until recently, emphasis was placed solely upon separation between mother and child. A greater appreciation of the importance of fathers with regard to child-rearing has now become apparent. For example, there is evidence that fathers provide role models for their sons in terms of appropriate masculine behavior. Boys without steady paternal influence may develop a distorted sense of what it means to be a man. This can take the form either of feminization or hyper-masculinity—super macho behavior that emulates a mythical rather than an actual masculine role model. (In the absence of the latter, some boys will imitate the actions and words of super-heroes of film or TV. Since behaving like the Hulk or Starsky and Hutch is not adaptive in the real world, this can lead to problems.)

Father's absence does not take place only when death or divorce occurs. Certain jobs and professions impose long or frequent separations. Corporate executives are often required to travel from city to city and may touch base with their families only on weekends. Long-distance truck drivers, salesmen, and physicians with specialities that place them on call for emergencies are also likely to be separated from spouses and children for extended periods.

One special case of father-child separation takes place among military personnel whose tours of duty may cause them to be gone for months at a time. There is some research indicating a higher than average rate of psychological problems among the children of career military people. This may be intensified by the difficulties, on the part of the officer or enlisted man, in separating military routine from family rules. Attempts to impose the rigid structure of the military system upon child-rearing can have disastrous results because such hyper-discipline does not take into account the innate differences that exist from child to child, nor the importance of allowing youngsters to develop at their own pace.

In the past, an executive's success was measured in terms of how often he became promoted. Each step up the corporate ladder was accompanied by a raise in salary and prestige and, quite often, a move to a new position in a new city. Business people functioning in this system ran the risk of losing sight of rewards emanating from family life and of concentrating only upon the payoff offered by The Company. It was unheard of to turn down a promotion merely because this meant that more hours would have to be spent away from the family. With increased attention to the paternal role in child-rearing, however, some fathers are reassessing their priorities and are deciding to forego some degree of professional advancement in favor of a more stable family environment.

The issue of maternal separation has become more relevant, too, because more and more mothers are joining the work force outside the home. Some of this has been ''blamed'' upon the feminist movement. However, in the vast majority of cases women work outside the home not because they are attempting to achieve psychological fulfillment but because economic necessities dictate it. The question has changed from "Is day-care acceptable as an alternative?" to "What type of day-care is best?" Psychological studies have failed to find evidence that children placed in good day-care centers suffer emotional or intellectual damage. This may reflect an actual lack of negative effects, or we may lack the scientific tools to measure these effects. A third possibility exists that there are negative side effects of day-care but that these do not begin to show themselves until years later. In any event, the question of the psychological benefits or detriments resulting from day-care is an open one.

Increasingly, children grow up in families where both parents work outside the home. This can begin while the child is still an infant. In such families, the child has the opportunity to make a gradual adjustment to separation and develops coping skills. Special problems may arise for the preschool youngster who is accustomed to having Mom at home and then must adapt to her decision to seek outside employment. When this is brought about by a situation involving additional stress, such as divorce or paternal illness, the trauma is magnified.

The child about to experience a new separation must be assured that he is not being punished for some wrong. Offer him an accurate explanation of the adult decision and the reasons behind it. Prepare him for the change well before it actually takes place. This will give him a chance to assimilate the news and vent feelings of anger, resentment, and fear of abandonment. Plan to spend extra time that is special with the child when you are home. When there is a choice, avoid having a new maternal separation coincide with an additional stress, such as beginning school. It is best to wait a month or so for the child to adjust to his school surroundings before embarking on still another major life change.

We have already discussed why children do not benefit from overly structured preschools or child-care centers. Working parents should also be aware that there are alternatives to day-care, such as providing a good babysitter—a consistent person to whom the child can become attached. This may be especially beneficial for the very young child. In the past, when families lived in rural settings and family members were enlisted for child-care support, this was a natural phenomenon. Aunts, grandmothers, and grandfathers became involved in bringing up children. Today, it may be necessary to hire an outside "specialist" to provide such care. Using a babysitter, as opposed to sending the child to a day-care center, has the advantage of providing continuity and security. On the other hand, much depends upon the personal attributes of the babysitter. An inappropriate sitter has the potential to inflict greater damage than an inappropriate day-care person; in the latter case, the child can find other sources of contact. The day-care center provides children with the opportunity to engage in group and peer activities—important for youngsters above the ages of three—and the play facilities are likely to be superior.

With a consistent babysitter there is the probability that the child may transfer affection and attachment away from parents to the sitter. This can prove threatening to many parents but is an understandable consequence of parent-child separation. Children will seek care where they can find it. Parents who take the time to make active and gratifying use of the time they do spend with their children reduce the risk of weakening the parent-child bond. In fact, the psychological connection between children and their parents is so strong that it takes an extraordinary amount of neglect, trauma, and hostility to threaten it seriously.

One of the most creative and attractive uses of day-care centers involves the location of child-care facilities at the place of work. This has not been done extensively in the United

States, but in Europe, many factories and places of business provide on-the-job child-care. This enables working parents to spend time with their children during lunch and other breaks and provides the security of physical proximity for youngsters and adults. Perhaps if the current trend toward having two parents working continues, increased demand for such facilities will bring about their existence in this country.

Issues of separation arise in any family—whether or not one or both parents work outside the home. The most common example of this has to do with parents taking vacations without the children. There is no hard and fast rule about when it is okay to do this, and much will depend upon the parent's feelings as well as those of the child. Most young children can tolerate an absence of two or three days if they are prepared for it beforehand and understand the reasons why mommy and daddy are going away. Specifically, youngsters need to know that they are not being punished, that they are still loved, and that their parents will return soon. In addition, children who have become accustomed since infancy to staying with other trusted adults—such as grandparents, aunts and uncles, or the parents' close friends—will find vacation separations easier. The youngster below the age of three or four who has never spent an extended period with anyone other than his mother or father is likely to be frightened by an initial separation. When parents do take brief vacations, they should call regularly—daily if this is possible—at consistent, predictable times. Extended vacations without the children are not recommended for parents of young children.

One special type of separation anxiety can occur when the preschool child is confronted with the arrival of a sibling. This is particularly true of youngsters below the age of three, who are more likely to be threatened by the loss of parents' attention.

Infants require a great deal of physical care and can easily monopolize attention. A new baby is also extremely appealing. Even though the older child has been prepared for his new brother or sister, he probably will express resentment and may even regress behaviorally. These are normal, usually short-lived reactions.

You can help the older child by actively engaging him in the infant-rearing process. Give him a definite role—that of parental helper—if he so wishes, and praise him for his competence. Find time to spend with him that is not related to the baby's care and assure him that the love being given to the baby has not been taken from him—he is still special to you.

10

Anxiety-Related Disorders

Since anxiety is a physiological as well as a psychological response, it is not surprising that increased tension can affect almost any part of the body. There may be children who are vulnerable to upsets in specific organ systems—cardiovascular, respiratory, intestinal, muscular—and such weaknesses may run in families. The tendency for similar anxiety disorders to occur in parents and children may be due to genetics, as well as to the fact that children imitate the anxious behavior of their parents. For example, the well-known finding that children who stutter are likely to have at least one parent or close relative who stutters may be due to an inborn trait and/or to modeling of non-fluent speech patterns.

The following are some of the more common anxiety-related disorders that occur in children. In contrast to overt fears, these problems represent instances where anxiety has an indirect effect upon behavior.

Headaches

Children who suffer from frequent headaches may do so for various reasons. In rare cases, persistent headaches may be due to brain damage or tumors. These so-called *organic* headaches are usually accompanied by intense, even blinding, pain, as well as nausea, vomiting, numbness, and double vision. Though organic headaches are not common, it is essential that any child with frequent headaches be seen by a physician for a complete medical checkup.

A second kind of headache that occurs in children results from an initial constriction (tightening) and subsequent dilation (expansion) of the blood vessels of the head. The most common of these *vascular* disorders are *migraine* or *cluster* headaches. Migraine and cluster headaches are often accompanied by nausea and vomiting and tend to begin on one side of the head behind the eye socket. These headaches run in families and sufferers have been labeled as perfectionistic and rigid. Such judgments, however, have not been based on clear scientific data.

Migraine headaches have been reported in children as young as five and are even suspected in infants. According to one study, approximately 5 percent of children between the ages of ten and twelve suffer from migraine headaches, with average age of onset at seven years. This figure was considered low. While adult migraine sufferers tend to be predominantly female, a slight *majority* of children with the disorder are males. A connection has been established between migraines and allergies. Certain foods, especially those rich in substances that affect the blood vessels (the most common of these is *tyramine*) have been suspected of aggravating headaches in individuals who are susceptible. Such edibles include cheese and other dairy products, chocolate, fish, beans, pork, citrus products, onions, wheat, and nuts. Migraines are also known to be aggravated by physical factors such as bright lights, loud noises, television, fatigue, as well as by emotional stress.

Vascular headaches can often be controlled through the use of chemicals that help constrict the blood vessels, diet, allergic desensitization, or a combination of these. There has been recent success in training adult and adolescent headache patients to bring about voluntary changes in the blood vessels by changing the temperature of the hand and transferring this to the scalp. In addition, voluntary control has been achieved through the use of imagery training. Although behavioral approaches have not been reported extensively for pediatric migraine patients, one would suspect that childrens' superior abilities to entertain vivid mental images would make them especially suited for training.

Beware of unqualified professionals—including psychologists and physicians—who recommend a cursory stab at "biofeedback" as part of a slickly packaged, headache treatment plan. Biofeedback is only a means of *providing information* to the patient in order to give him positive payoff for successful relaxation. The essential element in this type of treatment is the learning of relaxation itself. Migraine headaches are not a problem that should be treated by anyone other than the trained specialist.

The child with migraine may need psychological counseling aimed at helping him to deal with stress. This may involve treatment for the entire family in which new patterns of coping with anxiety-provoking events are learned. While such treatment cannot cause migraine headaches to disappear, it may reduce their frequency.

The most common type of childhood headache is the *tension headache,* which results from prolonged tightening of the muscles of the scalp, face, and neck. In order to illustrate how tension leads to pain, try a simple exercise. Take one hand and tighten it up into a fist. Hold it, as tightly as possible, for thirty seconds. Keep going for another thirty. What begins to happen? The hand starts to ache. Now imagine what that hand would feel if it remained clenched for several hours at a time.

The muscles of the face, neck, and scalp are physiologically no different from those of the hands. Keeping them tight for more than a brief period of time causes fatigue and pain. The difference is that while we are usually aware of making a fist, we can tighten up our head and neck muscles for quite a while without knowing it. The result is what the television commercials call a "simple nervous tension headache." (Their solution to this problem—taking an aspirin, buffered or otherwise—makes no sense, however. The key is to learn how to *avoid* tight scalp muscles, not to constantly mask the pain!)

Anything that brings about tightening of the head muscles can lead to headaches. This can be something totally innocuous—such as squinting or looking into the sun too long—or it can result from emotional factors. The child who experiences anxiety-provoking thoughts or events may react by tightening up his muscles as part of a generalized response. After he allows his other muscles to relax, his neck, face, and scalp muscles may remain taut.

When a child complains of frequent headaches for which no organic reason can be found, it is best to check out a few, nonpsychological factors before examining the existence of emotional causes for this problem:

Is the child reading in a poor light, causing him to squint?

Is he playing in the sun without proper protection?

Have his eyes been checked for myopia (near sightedness) or other visual problems that can be corrected with prescription eyeglasses?

Do the headaches occur after the child has eaten a certain food, indicating a possible allergic reaction?

In the absence of any of the above, it is reasonable to assume that the headaches are the result of increased anxiety in one or more aspects of the youngster's life. School worries are a frequent cause of headaches, particularly concerns over getting good grades. This is most likely to happen in families where unusually high standards are set and where perfectionism is practiced.

Talking to the child in an attempt to find out what is bothering him is the first step. Once the source of anxiety has been found, the headaches may respond to simple reassurance and support. Parents should also examine whether the child has observed someone in the family, or close to it, who suffers from frequent headaches and gets a lot of extra attention because of this problem. While a child's suffering deserves a sympathetic response, parents should ensure that youngsters are not relieved of chores and responsibilities because of headaches. Their aim should be to avoid major disruption of the family schedule.

The child under the age of six with frequent tension headaches can be helped by learning to imagine going to a favorite place and using this imagery the minute a headache begins to come on. For example, visualizing going to the beach or an amusement park—somewhere that has proved pleasurable and meaningful for him—will often bring about heavy, regular breathing and quick loosening of the muscles of the scalp and face. This teaches the child a relaxation response that is incompatible with anxiety. The key is to guide the child in doing this at the earliest signs of pain so that he is likely to succeed. In addition, suggestions can be made that he will feel in charge and in control.

I have also been able to teach preschool children to visualize their headache as a monster or bad guy. The "headache monster" can then be drawn on a piece of paper, torn up, and thrown out. In this way, anger is used in a constructive manner. Frequently, combining the ''headache monster'' approach along with imagery works extremely well.

Older children can benefit from learning progressively to relax the muscles of face, scalp, and neck, as well as from pleasant imagery. This can be done through an exercise I call the ''Prune.'' The following case illustrates how the Prune is used.

Kenny, an eleven-year-old boy, was referred to me because of daily headaches for which no medical reason was found. Of interest was the fact that his father also suffered from headaches. (I have found a very high percentage of children with chronic headaches to have parents with the same problem.) After speaking to Kenny, it became clear that he was reacting to stress in two major areas. First, he had moved to a new school and was experiencing a lot of teasing from his classmates. Second, the move had forced him to share a room with a younger brother. The two boys fought constantly over territory, belongings, and numerous other issues. Kenny's parents were adding a new room to the house so that he would have his own sleeping quarters. This would not be completed for several months, however, and until that time the sibling conflict was likely to persist.

In order to handle his schoolmates' teasing, Kenny was trained in extinguishing undesirable behavior through the use of the Science Experiment technique. Nevertheless, it would take some time before he would be able to eliminate this annoying conduct, and his tension was likely to continue. Coupled with the troubles he was having with his brother, this would probably result in continued headaches. For this reason, a direct approach was taken, and Kenny was taught to relax using the following series of tense-relax exercises:

1. Make a fist and hold it tight for seven seconds.
2. Relax the hand for a (silent) count of twenty, concen-

trating on the loose, heavy feeling of the relaxed muscles.

3. Tighten the muscles of the forehead for seven seconds by raising the eyebrows high.

4. Relax forehead muscles for count of twenty.

5. Tense cheek muscles for seven seconds by smiling as widely as possible.

6. Relax cheek muscles, let mouth hang slightly open for count of twenty.

7. Tense jaw muscles by clenching teeth. Seven seconds.

8. Relax jaw muscles. Twenty seconds.

9. Tense nose muscles by wrinkling nose for seven seconds.

10. Relax nose muscles. Twenty seconds.

11. Tense eye muscles by clamping eyes tightly shut. Seven seconds.

12. Relax eye muscles. May keep eyes closed. Twenty seconds.

13. Tighten neck muscles by dropping head back to shoulders. Seven seconds.

14. Relax neck muscles. Let head hang foreward loosely. Twenty seconds.

15. Now the entire face, as well as head and neck are totally relaxed. At the count of three, tense up all muscles at the same time—forehead, cheeks, jaw, nose, eyes, and neck. Scrunch up entire face, making it tight and wrinkled, *just like a prune.* One, two, three: Tighten. Hold for count of seven.

16. Relax all muscles, breathing comfortably. Remain relaxed.

After a few practice sessions, Kenny was able to relax deeply merely by doing the two-step Prune part of the exercise. He tightened up all of his muscles, held for seven seconds, then totally relaxed them. He was instructed to do this at least twice a day—upon waking and before going to bed—and any time he started to feel a headache coming on or found himself in an anxiety-provoking situation. I suggested to him that he imagine a pleasant scene while feeling relaxed and that he use this scene to make anxious feelings go away. Kenny chose an imaginary camping trip with his father as his favorite scene.

Within two weeks, Kenny achieved excellent control over his headaches. The situations that caused him to be anxious had not changed. However, he had learned to cope with them and had mastered the method of relaxing his head muscles in order to prevent most headaches, as well as reduce the intensity of the ones that did occur. His mother reported that he did his "headache exercises" frequently and that she had suggested that her husband try this method for his own problem.

Relaxation exercises such as the Prune can be used with adolescents and youngsters who have the patience and attention span, as well as the motivation, to sit through a training session similar to the one described above. Children under the age of nine or ten are unlikely to be so patient; they benefit more from approaches that emphasize imagery along with suggestions of warmth, heaviness, and comfort of the facial muscles.

Some of my headache patients have been highly motivated, hard-driving, preteens and adolescents who develop pain after long sessions of homework or studying for exams. These young people benefit from being taught to use time wisely and moderately. Instead of studying for three straight hours, they should be guided into dividing up the evening into three one hour sessions. After each hour, they can receive suggestions to stop, take a fifteen-minute break, and reward themselves for studying—by listening to a record, having a snack, or chatting with a friend on the phone. Students who are especially hard-driving often have a tendency to punish themselves for success by adding on more work. Completion of the first batch of homework brings about an immediate forging ahead into the second batch, and then the third, until exhaustion and muscle fatigue set in. It is surprising how difficult it is for such young people to learn to reward themselves.

Stomachaches

In order to propel food through the digestive system, the stomach and intestines undergo a continuous, wavelike movement called *peristalsis*. Increased anxiety has the effect of speeding up the rate of peristaltic activity. Because of this, children and adults under stress experience "butterflies in the stomach" or, in more severe cases, nausea and vomiting. A second way that anxiety affects the gastrointestinal system is by increasing the flow of hydrochloric acid to the stomach. This can bring about stomachaches. An extreme example of the damaging impact of anxiety upon the stomach occurs when the concentration of acid becomes sufficiently high to cause a sore, or ulcer, in the lining of the stomach. Ulcers are often brought about by nonpsychological factors, and there appears to be a tendency in certain people to develop them. There is little doubt, though, that emotional stress is a contributing factor both in causing stomach ulcers and in making an existing ulcer worse.

The child who experiences chronic stomach pain for which no medical reason can be found may be especially vulnerable to developing chronic abdominal problems, such as ulcers, in adulthood. Continuous or frequent stomachaches as well as chronic vomiting of unexplained origin are a strong sign that the youngster is experiencing environmental stress and is coping with this in a particularly painful way. Children who are perfectionistic and set unrealistically high standards for themselves seem to be at high risk for such psychosomatic disorders.

In 1958, Dr. Joseph Brady conducted an experiment that shed some light on the psychological processes behind the development of ulcers. Dr. Brady had two sets of monkeys hooked up to a series of electrical monitoring devices. The first group received regularly scheduled electric shocks. The second group, which Brady labeled the "executive monkeys," was responsible for preventing the first group from receiving the shocks. Brady found that it was the group of executives, not the victims, who developed increased rates of peptic ulcers. Replication of this study in 1963 with college students, in which the rate of gastric activity was measured, produced similar results.

While it is difficult to generalize directly from laboratory studies with animals and adults to children, the "executive monkey" study suggests that children who feel overburdened with responsibility and the need to make frequent, important decisions may be at risk for abdominal problems. Children should of course be given responsibility, but their obligations and chores should be proportional to their age and developmental level. Specifically, boys should not be treated as "little men" nor should girls be treated as "little women." Neither should be given the roles of surrogate spouses.

Youngsters with chronic abdominal pain should be seen for professional psychological treatment. This may involve both an exploration and resolution of the stress that is going on in the child's life as well as training in relaxation that can help prevent or reduce distress. Imagery techniques that involve the visualization of cool and refreshing scenes are often helpful. Some doctors make use of very direct imagery, in which the patient learns to visualize his stomach. During anxious states, he is instructed to see the organ as a red, hot sack, while during relaxation, he watches it pale to a peaceful, tranquil white. The patient practices seeing the stomach go through these changes—from red to pink to white—and gains control over this imaginary process. Theoretically, actual physical change will take place simultaneously. The use of such guided imagery for various types of chronic pain has proved helpful for many patients.

Tooth Grinding

Children who wake up in the morning and complain of a sore jaw are likely to be grinding their teeth in their sleep. A dental examination in which the surfaces of the teeth are found to be abraded can easily confirm this. Often parents will be able to hear the sound of enamel grinding against enamel as they pass by the sleeping youngster's room. The technical term for such behavior is *bruxism*. Tooth-grinding can cause dental problems as well as considerable jaw, head and neck pain.

As is the case with any other anxiety-related disorder, the child who bruxes needs to be evaluated for sources of elevated stress in his environment. Perhaps there are specific fears, worries, or bad dreams that plague him at night that can be allayed by explanation, assurance, and comfort. The approach advised for children with insomnia and night fears—making sure that bedtime is a peaceful, relaxing part of the youngster's day—is beneficial for youngsters who grind their teeth. In addition, training in relaxing the muscles of the jaw can be especially helpful in reducing bruxism.

In order to accomplish this, the child should be offered the explanation that his jaw pain results from grinding his teeth at night, that other children do the same thing, and that this is certainly not his fault. However, he can be told, this can be helped by learning how to loosen the muscles of the jaw before falling asleep. In order to achieve best results, muscle relaxation training should take place with the child in bed, just before lights out.

Suggestions should be offered to lie comfortably, breathe slowly and comfortably, and think of a pleasant or favorite scene. As this takes place and the youngster's respiration becomes rhythmic, the following exercises can be done:

1. Smile as widely as possible for (silent) count of seven.
2. Relax, letting mouth hang open slightly, concentrating on how comfortable the lips and mouth feel. Count of twenty.
3. Repeat 1 and 2.
4. Clench jaws tightly for count of seven.
5. Relax, letting jaws grow warm, and heavy, and comfortable. Count of twenty.
6. Repeat 4 and 5.
7. Continue to think of pleasant scene and become even more comfortable, concentrating upon how relaxed and heavy the whole face feels. Now you can have a pleasant night's sleep.

As is true of any relaxation exercise suggested in this book, this should only be undertaken with the child's enthusiastic agreement and only by a parent who is relaxed and comfortable and at ease with this process. If bedtime is set up as an especially positive time of day, relaxation training will be greatly enhanced.

Children who grind their teeth can also be aided by suggestions that they practice tightening and loosening their jaw muscles throughout the day. This can be done unobtrusively and teaches the child to be more aware of when he is expressing tension in this particular manner. As youngsters grow more sensitive about differentiating tense and relaxed muscle states, they become more able to control this process.

It is helpful to encourage children suffering from bruxism or any other type of psychosomatic anxiety problem to express their feelings verbally as well, since this offers a more constructive way to deal with the inevitable frustrations of life than the self-punishment that results from pain and discomfort.

Asthma

Asthma is a condition that results from an oversensitivity of the respiratory system to physical or emotional stimulation or a combination of these. During an asthmatic attack, the bronchial tubes narrow. This cuts off the air supply to the lungs and brings about wheezing and difficulty in breathing. Asthma may result from infection or an allergic reaction, or it may be triggered by anxiety and stress. It is probably genetically influenced, although there are many asthmatics who have no family history of this problem. Twice as many boys as girls suffer from asthma, and it is essentially, a disorder of young people, with 60 percent of all asthmatics falling below the age of seventeen.

It is safe to say that psychological factors, such as anxiety and fear, are not sufficient *by themselves* to bring about an asthmatic attack. However in children with tendencies toward allergies, chronic bronchitis, chest colds, or penumonia, the respiratory system may be a prime target for psychosomatic problems. Research conducted by Dr. Kenneth Purcell and his associates at the Children's Asthma Research Institute and Hospital (CARIH) in Denver, Colorado, indicates that a large proportion of severely asthmatic children lose their symptoms without any medication when they leave their homes. While Dr. Purcell did find a group of youngsters who did not improve unless continuous dosages of steroid drugs were administered, the rest of the patients he studied remained symptom-free for periods as long as two years without medical treatment. The drug-free youngsters were more likely to report asthma attacks following emotional unheaval than were the patients who required medication. This indicates the importance of considering both physical and psychological environments when evaluating the asthmatic child.

Some doctors have put forth the notion of an "asthmatic personality." According to this theory, asthma is symbolic of suppressed crying. However, there is no systematic scientific data to support this idea and experts such as Dr. Purcell have pointed out that if the child with asthma cries less than other youngsters it may be because he has learned that crying can trigger an attack. Thus, not crying may very well be an adaptive coping mechanism, not evidence of an emotional problem. Similarly, researchers who have shown that children with asthma tend to be more anxious and depressed than their healthy peers have no way of separating out whether the anxiety causes asthma or whether being chronically ill causes heightened anxiety.

Asthma is a medical condition that needs to be monitored closely by a physician. Along with medical care, serious attention needs to be paid to psychological issues in the child's life. I recall one asthmatic patient of mine, a thirteen-year-old boy, whose parents were constantly fighting. When he began to wheeze or show other signs of an attack, the marital conflict ceased and all attention was focused upon him. After his parents received marriage counseling and their fights decreased, so did the asthmatic attacks. This does not imply that this boy's asthma was "fake." It is very important to understand that psychologically induced attacks are as real as those brought about by infections or allergic reactions and that the pain and suffering experienced by the child is every bit as severe. However, physical events can be conditioned to occur in the presence of certain psychological stimuli.

Relaxation approaches aimed at inducing rhythmic breathing and loose, heavy muscles have been shown to bring symptomatic relief for many children with asthma. Such treatment should be conducted by a trained professional. In order to increase the probability of success the psychologist will discuss with the patient, in detail, the environmental factors that appear related to attacks. He may ask the child to record if symptoms occur at a certain time of day, during specific weather conditions, in specific places, or during particular emotional states. With such information, the psychologist can tailor the treatment to the individual needs of the child. For example, if he finds that eleven-year-old Laurie's asthma flares up in the evening, after six o'clock he can instruct her to practice relaxation exercises at a quarter to six and, perhaps, prevent attacks or reduce their severity.

For the child who is experiencing high levels of conflict or stress, psychotherapy can be of help. (In most cases, approaches that work on directly teaching relaxation should be included.) Treatment may be individual or it may involve the entire family. As is the case with many chronic diseases, asthma affects not only the sufferer but his siblings and parents as well. Mothers and fathers may blame themselves for "causing" the child's problem. They may view themselves as genetic "carriers" or may feel that they have emotionally upset the child. Brothers and sisters may be afraid of catching asthma or may resent the special attention received by the child due to his attacks. This last factor brings us to an important point—the need to maintain as normal a life as possible for both the child with asthma and his family.

Some asthmatic youngsters require long-term hospitalization. The majority can be medically managed with steroid drugs and psychological support and are able to live at home, go to school, and lead normal lives. An asthmatic attack is a frightening event for parents, who watch in horror as the child struggles to breathe, gasping and wheezing. In a few cases asthma can prove fatal. Thus it is quite easy to overprotect the asthmatic child and afford him the opportunity to get out of chores that his siblings must continue to do. This creates a danger that children will learn to use their symptoms as a tool for avoiding obligations and responsibility. Parents should communicate closely with the physician and find out exactly what restrictions upon activities must be observed. These should be followed closely. Twelve-year-old Seth may begin to wheeze and experience an asthma attack after being asked to take out the garbage. Rather than drop the issue permanently, his parents may find it useful to assist him in getting through the attack and, when he is breathing comfortably, tell him "Now that you're feeling okay, you can go take out the garbage." In general, most children can learn to manage their own symptoms through the use of inhalers and relaxation exercises, so that direct parental intervention is not necessary. Understandably, mothers and fathers will be on the alert for signs of a severe or dangerous attack. In the absence of these, however, it is best to encourage as much self-reliance and independence as possible.

Stuttering

Stuttering, or stammering (the terms are identical and interchangeable), is the result of anxiety associated with the process of speaking. There is little evidence of any physical component to this speech disorder. The mouths, throats, larynges, tongues, and lips of children who stutter are structurally no different from those of fluent youngsters. Stuttering is much more common in boys than in girls (estimates run from three to eight times more common, which may be due to the fact that verbal skills seem to develop more rapidly in girls than in boys.) It is familial to the extent that children who stutter are likely to have a parent or close relative with the same problem. This is probably the result of imitation.

There are different types of stuttering. Some children may repeat a sound or syllable (bouncing); others may have difficulty in forcing out words (choking); still others may stretch sounds (sliding); and there are youngsters who exhibit more than one of these patterns. All such difficulties are known as *blocking*.

Most children who stutter do not do so all the time. The proportions of fluent and blocked speech vary widely from child to child, and, for a given child, from time to time. Some youngsters are fluent 90 percent of the time and experience problems only in isolated situations. Others have difficulty speaking almost constantly. The frequency and intensity of stuttering can be increased by subjecting the child to stress. Stuttering is frequently associated with public speaking, talking before large groups, addressing individuals whom the child feels are passing judgment on him or are otherwise seen as intimidating, and talking on the telephone. It is rare for children to stutter while singing or engaging in group recital.

There is, as yet, no effective cure for stuttering. The best way to approach this highly embarrassing problem is to *prevent it*.

Virtually all of us lose fluency when we are under stress. What separates the stutterer from the non-stutterer is the frequency of this behavior. Most children go through periods, between the ages of two and five, when they hesitate, stutter, or in some other way show loss of speech fluency. *This is normal and will go away by itself if left alone.* Parents should ignore such acute or *primary* stuttering and not bring it to the child's attention. Mothers and fathers who ridicule a young child who is having difficulty expressing himself or who incessantly correct him, interrupt him, finish sentences for him, advise him to take a deep breath and slow down, or in any other way call excessive attention to the process of speech run the risk of transforming temporary, primary loss of fluency into chronic, *secondary* stuttering. This is because the child exposed to such treatment quickly *learns to pay attention to how he is talking rather than to what he is talking about.* Such internal scrutiny creates confusion, hesitation, and anxiety. Each time the child stutters he becomes more and more anxious about talking. Anxiety tightens up the muscles of the throat and impedes the normal flow of air and sound. As negative associations build upon each other, a long-term disorder is created.

Imagine what it would be like if you had to measure and consider each word before it left your mouth! *For speech to be fluent, it needs to be automatic.* The same is true of other motor behaviors such as writing or driving a car. When we first learn such activities, we must pay attention to every little nuance—exactly how to make the letter ''a'' look like an ''a,'' precisely how hard to touch the brake to make a car stop without plunging us through the windshield. Soon, these skills become well integrated into our sensory-motor system; if we then stop to think about them, we encounter difficulties. The key to preventing stuttering is not to make a big deal about speech. This approach should also be followed when dealing with the child who is a chronic stutterer.

Pay attention to what the child says, not how he says it. Don't grimace, turn away, or in any other way indicate disapproval to the youngster who is blocking. Don't interrupt or give advice on how to talk more effectively. Speech therapy, while quite useful for children with structural impediments such as lisping or enunciation problems, is generally not helpful for the stuttering child. Of course the speech therapist who creates good emotional rapport with the child may, by virtue of making him feel relaxed, help him speak more fluently. However this has more to do with good interpersonal skills and emotional sensitivity than with the specific techniques of speech therapy, per se.

Among American Indian tribes who use very relaxed methods of child-rearing, *stuttering does not exist*. In fact, the languages of these tribes have no word for stuttering. Parents living in cultures that are (supposedly) more sophisticated or "developed" would do well to take guidance from this.

The child who stutters must feel he has ample time and opportunity to say what is on his mind. Activities and situations that promote and enhance higher self-esteem will contribute toward greater fluency of speech. Some children who frequently stutter can be quite fluent while discussing a topic about which they feel knowledgeable. Similarly, some parents have observed that youngsters who stutter are unusually fluent when talking to younger children. In these cases, feelings of control lead to ease of verbal communication.

Dr. Joseph Sheehan of UCLA has developed a technique that helps many stutterers. It involves teaching the individual to stutter and feel comfortable about it. Dr. Sheehan's patients are trained to stutter voluntarily and to accept "bouncing," "choking," and "sliding" as okay. In this way, the process of speech loses some of its forbidding anxiety-provoking qualities and the stutterer gains more control over his vocal output. Dr. Sheehan's approach does not actually lead to a "cure" or total elimination of stuttering, but it has helped many individuals engage more comfortably in everyday social and professional activities.

Even for the child who has become a chronic stutterer—this is usually apparent once the youngster has reached the age of seven—there is hope. If he can be helped to boost his self-esteem, and if unusual amounts of stress are not imposed upon him, the childhood stutterer will usually experience increased fluency by adolescence.

Stuttering is a problem to which the old adage "Discretion is the better part of valor" applies. What parents do is less important than what they do *not* do. Left alone, the speech patterns of most children, even those who seem to be experiencing difficulties between the ages of two and five, will work themselves out. When exposed to criticism or excessive scrutiny, even the most fluent young child can learn to become chronically anxious about each word that leaves his lips.

Anxiety Attacks

Sudden episodes of anxiety occur three or four times more frequently in girls than in boys. Such attacks, which begin abruptly and seem unrelated to anything in the child's current life, are most common before the onset of puberty. They may be accompanied by feelings of intense terror and panic as well as bodily symptoms such as rapid heartbeat, heavy breathing, flushing, and dizziness—the classical signs of anxiety.

The particular tendency of girls to experience anxiety attacks raises an interesting speculation. The relationship between sex-roles and the expression of anxiety in children was touched upon in chapter 1, and it was suggested that girls may feel free to express fear overtly while boys communicate distress in a more covert manner. Though the difference in behavior may in part be attributable to hormones, it may also result from early sex-role stereotyping that conditions females to be passive, helpless, and unable to assert themselves. Anxiety attacks are the epitome of helplessness, a state that has been rewarded for the female but not the male.

Though anxiety attacks may appear to be without basis,

psychological investigation usually reveals a previous trauma in the child's life. Acute episodes of anxiety can appear in youngsters who have undergone surgery without adequate preparation. A death in the family or witnessing of unusual or frightening experiences, such as a crime or serious accident, have also been implicated as possible contributing factors. Some researchers have contended that timid, high-strung, serious-minded, conscientious children are especially prone to sudden attacks of anxiety.

Anxiety attacks are not a separate problem, in and of themselves. They are, indeed, examples of a generalized, bodily reaction to threat. The stress that brings them about can relate to any number of experiences or fears. It is important that children who exhibit anxiety attacks receive psychological help as quickly as possible. Because of their acute, dramatic, and frightening nature, anxiety attacks, like asthma, have the potential to generate a tremendous amount of concern and attention among family members. Alarmed parents may allow the child to learn to use his attacks as a way of enforcing his will upon others. This can set the stage for a lifetime pattern of "unhealthy power"—attaining success through helplessness and illness rather than through competence and assertion.

Psychotherapy—which, in many cases, need not be lengthy—can aid the child in finding out what events and objects are causing him to have the seemingly random attacks. Once the anxiety-provoking stimuli are recognized, a repertoire of anti-anxiety strategies can be developed to help in unlearning the fearful response.

In cases where immediate relief from anxiety is necessary, pediatricians may prescribe a tranquilizer, such as Benadryl. Calming medications are highly effective in the short run. However they serve only as temporary sources of comfort and will have little lasting effect in the absence of meaningful change in the child's emotional environment. Other factors to consider when evaluating the use of tranquilizers for children are the possibility of drug dependence and the fact that many children do not like the way they feel while under the influence of such medications.

11

Toilet Problems

In traditional Hebraic law, certain crimes or transgressions were punished by public flogging. The Jewish Talmud notes, however, that in cases where the convicted criminal experiences loss of bowel or bladder continence due to fear, he need not be flogged. Presumably, the loss of control was assumed to be sufficient punishment.

The tendency for fear and distress to reduce excretory control is not limited to intellectually sophisticated human animals nor is it a by-product of extensive thought. Rather it is a sudden, inborn response common to most mammals. For example, laboratory animals who have received strong doses of electric shock or have been subjected to other forms of severe stress will almost always respond by urinating and defecating. Many pet owners have noted similar occurrences even in well-trained domestic animals.

While loss of control is a sudden reaction, learning to develop voluntary mastery over excretory processes means delaying gratification—interrupting a physical reflex. As such, it requires training.

Voluntary control over urination and defecation is learned.

In the case of the former, the bladder fills with urine and stimulates nerves that send a message to the brain. The brain decodes this, interprets it as "Time to let go," and sends back a message to the nerves that trigger the bladder to release the surplus fluid. In human infants, this process is automatic and proceeds without delay. When the baby feels the urge to urinate, he does so. As he becomes "trained," the child learns to interrupt the response chain. The brain decodes: "Wait. Let go at appropriate time and place."

A similar process takes place during defecation, except that the organ of storage is the lowest part of the large intestine—the bowel. Both bladder and bowel are strong, highly elastic organs whose outer muscles, called *sphincters,* can be brought under voluntary control, through training.

Human babies at birth are not sufficiently developed to be able to control their sphincter muscles. Just as the process of increased mastery and control occurs in all other aspects of the infant's development, so it applies to toilet function. Attempts to toilet train a baby who is not physically ready are futile. Parents may hear stories of wondrous babies who were totally bowel and bladder trained at the age of ten months. While this precocity may occur in a small number of cases, careful questioning may reveal that what the proud parent meant by "trained" was that the child allowed himself to be carried to the commode at the time he was relieving himself.

Surprisingly, parents cannot always take credit for toilet training their children; *many children train themselves* when they are ready. The actual learning process is surprisingly rapid in a child who is sufficiently developed. This usually occurs no earlier than eighteen months of age and quite normally as late as three years. Drs. Nathan Azrin and Richard Foxx have demonstrated rapid toilet training with mentally retarded youngsters and have written an excellent guide to training children in a matter of hours (see Selected Readings, p. 275).

Some physically healthy children take longer to learn toilet control than others. The fact that toilet problems tend to run in families supports the notion that certain individuals are inherently prone to such difficulties. There is no relationship between intelligence and toilet training except at the extreme ends of the scale. Very intelligent youngsters tend to train themselves earlier, while developmentally slow children may also be slow in the attainment of voluntary toilet skills. There are, however, numerous bright and precocious youngsters who are slow to train, and parents should not regard slowness of learning within the normal range (eighteen to thirty-six months) as a sign of anything problematic.

While problems of toileting—bedwetting, constipation, and soiling—can occur in children who have never learned to be fully in control (called *primary* bedwetters and soilers) a more frequent pattern is that of the child who has learned to master going to the bathroom but who for some reason loses control. Such *secondary* difficulties are often due to anxiety and fear.

Because problems of toileting can easily result from an organic or structural problem, it is essential that any child with a history of bedwetting, constipation, or soiling receive a comprehensive physical examination to rule out medical factors. This may mean that the youngster's pediatrician will refer him to a specialist, such as a urologist or gastroenterologist for diagnostic tests. In cases where there is a structural defect, minor surgery can often quickly correct the problem. In the majority of cases no physical problem is found.

In our culture, great importance is attached to the process of excretion, which is viewed as somewhat revolting. The haste with which many parents move to promote early toilet training is evidence of the distaste we have for handling the feces or urine of another person, even those of our own children. Because of this, children who experience difficulty maintaining control over toilet behaviors are likely to feel extremely guilty, ashamed, or embarrassed. They may view themselves as babyish or encounter ridicule from peers (''Stinky,'' ''Wetpants''). Aside from the obvious need to treat children with compassion and understanding, the fact that shame promotes further anxiety and subsequent loss of control means that we should:

Never embarrass, demean, or in any way shame the child who has a toilet problem.

Except in rare cases, children do not wet the bed or soil their pants voluntarily.

Bedwetting

The most common toilet problem is bedwetting, or, as it is technically known, *enuresis*. The child who continues to wet the bed consistently after the age of four is considered to be enuretic. The word *consistent* is important because most healthy children occasionally lose control of their bladder. Studies have shown that about 15 percent of children chronically wet the bed. Thus, it is far from a rare disorder. The problem runs in families, with about a third of fathers of bedwetting children reporting a pattern of childhood enuresis and about a fifth of mothers recalling a similar history. This evidence of a probable genetic factor is supported by the finding that Israeli kibbutz children reared apart from their parents in communal nurseries showed the same family tendency to bed-wet.

There are several theories regarding the causes of enuresis. Some doctors, primarily those writing from a psychoanalytic point of view, have viewed this problem as essentially psychiatric in nature and as a symptom of some underlying psychic conflict. Specifically, children who wet the bed are seen as having troubles asserting themselves. Letting urine flow, uncontrolled, is seen as a form of passive behavior and as a sign of the child's reluctance to take control. While some psychoanalytic studies have indicated that children who wet the bed had other psychological problems, these were not scientifically controlled research endeavors and thus were open to the old cause-effect question. *There is little evidence to support the idea that bedwetting children are inevitably neurotic or psychologically abnormal.* Some children who wet the bed do have other emotional difficulties, but *most enuretics are normal.* Of course the guilt and shame that results from this problem may cause a loss of self-esteem or may otherwise restrict the child's social growth.

Most enuresis occurs at night. There is some evidence that children with a tendency to bedwet are extremely *deep sleepers.* They may not be able to receive the signal from the bladder to the brain fast enough or in sufficient strength to wake up to void. As mentioned earlier, bedwetters are also prone to two other conditions related to unusually deep sleep—sleepwalking and night terrors (these three symptoms have been referred to, lightheartedly, as the Nocturnal Triangle). Thus the genetic tendency involved in enuresis may be one of deep sleep as opposed to any defect in the urinary system.

Others have considered bedwetting to be the result of a faulty pattern of toilet training. In some cases, trauma during training can lead to fears and anxieties about going to the bathroom. For example, children trained without a potty chair can develop fears of falling into the toilet bowl. However, in the majority of instances, the toilet training history of children with enuresis is no more traumatic or in any way different from that of their non-bedwetting peers. In addition, since many children end up training themselves, it is clear that extensive teaching or training is not usually necessary to develop normal toilet skills. Despite this parents should certainly avoid coercive or anxiety-provoking methods of toilet training, for such techniques do no good.

There are several treatment approaches for enuresis. The anti-depressant drug *imipramine* (Tofranil) has been shown to significantly reduce the rate of bedwetting in many children. Researchers are unclear as to why this compound, originally developed to improve the mood of adult psychiatric patients, should have this effect. Some doctors have suggested that imipramine acts to alter the child's sleep pattern, while others have said that it may serve to relax the enuretic youngster. There are two main problems with administering imipramine for bedwetting. First, in many cases when the drug is discontinued, the enuresis returns. Second, like any drug, imipramine causes side effects such as irritability, nighttime restlessness, increased blood pressure, and slight weight loss.

A study by Dr. John Werry and his associates at the School of Medicine, University of New Zealand, revealed that in about 5 percent of cases, children whose bedwetting was reduced after taking imipramine showed deteriorated behavior. Dr. Werry also noted a tendency to administer amounts of the drug that exceeded the recommended dosage. He raised the point that bedwetting is a problem that is usually self-limiting—it eventually goes away by itself before adolescence. The advisability of giving children a potentially harmful medication for prolonged periods needs to be seriously weighed against the significance of the "cure."

Since there are other approaches that have proved useful in reducing or getting rid of enuresis that do not employ the use of drugs, I feel that imipramine should be used as a last resort and not as the first treatment of choice.

Dr. O. Hobart Mowrer, a prominent psychologist, considers the problem of nocturnal bedwetting a disorder of learning. For some unknown reason—deep sleep, constitutional muscle weakness, etc.—the betwetting child does not awaken when his bladder fills up. In other words, he has not learned the association between the sensation of fullness and waking. In an effort to help children learn this association, Dr. Mowrer invented a *conditioning device* known as a *bell and pad*.

This device consists of a pad that is attached to the bed. When urine touches the pad, an electric circuit is completed that causes a bell to ring. This wakes the child, and he is able to go to the bathroom to urinate. Numerous studies have shown the bell and pad to be effective in 90 percent of cases or more and it has been demonstrated to be significantly superior to psychotherapy. Despite this, bell and pad devices are not widely used.

Some of the reluctance to utilize a mechanical, electric device stems from misconceptions about the true nature of the bell and pad. Many parents and doctors mistakenly believe it to be an instrument of punishment that delivers an electric shock to the child. This is not so. The purpose of the bell and pad is not to punish the child for wetting but rather to rouse him so that his body learns the association between having to urinate and being awake and in control. Of course, care must be taken to purchase a bell and pad device that is mechanically sound. Parents should not use a conditioning device without first consulting a qualified physician or psychologist.

Conditioning devices should not be forced on any child, nor should they be used on a youngster who does not understand what is being attempted or who refuses to cooperate. Utilizing the bell and pad in such an inappropriate manner would, indeed, constitute punishment. Children should be given a full and accurate explanation about why their parents want to try the device. They should be reassured that it will not hurt them and that it is designed to help them be more in control. If they resist being awakened or have objections, the plan to utilize the bell and pad should be dropped.

Some doctors advise parents to wake the child during the night so that he can go to the bathroom. However, it is hard for parents to gauge exctly when the child wets, and they often end up waking the child after it is too late. Some parents find it inconvenient to stay up at night in order to wake the child. The bell and pad offers precision because it is triggered to go off the moment urination begins. Possible problems can arise, however, with a child who perspires heavily and whose body moisture sets off the bell. Readjusting the device may help, as can keeping the child's room cool at night.

For children who do not respond to the bell and pad, some doctors favor the use of urinary exercises. The premise behind this technique is that the bedwetting child has weak bladder sphincters. The exercises involve having the child practice stopping and resuming the flow of urination in midstream, several times a day. The object is to increase muscular control. Some success has been reported using this technique.

Another approach involves rewarding the child for dry nights. This can be used by itself or in conjunction with other therapies. The parents explain to the child that they know he is not wetting the bed on purpose and that wetting is not his fault. Nevertheless, they think it's great when he is able to stay dry, and they feel this is something that should be rewarded. The child keeps a chart and is given a reward the morning following each dry night. The reason why this often works is unclear; it may be that in instances where extreme anxiety contributes to lowered control, earning a reward serves as an enemy of anxiety. Since bedwetting children are often ashamed of their problem despite adult reassurance, they may want to keep their progress chart hidden and not discuss it with anyone other than the parent. Once again, it needs to be stressed that a reward system should not be foisted upon an unwilling child. Excessive parental zeal communicates to the youngster that his problem is terribly serious and that it really bothers Mom and Dad.

Children who respond favorably to the reward system will usually do so quickly. Once a consistent pattern of dry nights has been reached for several weeks, parents can start to "thin out" the reward schedule by requesting the child to be dry for two nights in a row in order to obtain his reward, then three, then four, etc., until the rewards are gradually faded out. Children will often spontaneously request that they no longer be paid for staying dry, since they no longer consider it a problem. This is a good sign that the child is feeling more in control.

No matter what specific treatment approach is used for bedwetting—imipramine, bell and pad, exercises, or rewards—there are some general issues that should be considered for all children with enuresis.

Some parents are careful to restrict the amount of fluids the child takes in before going to sleep. This is a waste of time. The child with normal bladder control can drink quarts and still wake up. The bedwetting youngster can take in a trickle and still wet. The problem is not the amount of fluid in the bladder but the integrity of the learned neuro-muscular response.

It is perfectly all right to request that the school-age bedwetting child change his own sheets, as long as this is not presented in an angry or punitive manner. Parents can explain that they are not upset with the child over his bedwetting, but feel he can change his own sheets because he is competent. This also reduces the risk of the child receiving an inordinate amount of attention because of his problem.

Parents should try never to get angry or frustrated at the youngster who wets the bed. Enuresis is, most probably, something that is out of the child's control. Having him change his own bedding allows him to avoid embarrassing confrontations and morning checking rituals accompanied by sighs of despair and sidelong glances. It helps maximize his privacy and dignity.

As we have mentioned, the vast majority of enuretic youngsters stop wetting the bed by adolescence. There will be children who do not respond to treatment of any kind. The best thing to do in such cases is *forget about it*. Avoid ridicule or making bedwetting a family issue. Provide reassurance, comfort, and a home environment that bolsters the child's sense of self-esteem. Consider all the many positive things that he accomplishes and attend to them. Resist thinking of him as a bedwetter but see him as a child who learns, plays, works, and goes through the normal everyday experience of childhood but who happens to have a specific problem that is likely to cure itself.

Though most enuresis occurs at night, there are a few children who wet during the day. These youngsters often speak of "forgetting" to go to the bathroom or of losing control over their bladder due to anxiety. Frequently, they were difficult to toilet train or may have never been trained completely. In many cases, daytime wetting is accompanied by soiling. A reward approach works best in these instances.

One additional note needs to be offered concerning the use of *hypnosis* for bedwetting. Hypnosis is not a parlor game or something that should be attempted at home. There is no doubt that hypnosis is a highly effective technique for bringing about behavior change when used by a competent professional. This will be discussed in detail in chapter 15 (Finding Professional Help).

Constipation and Stool Retention

Children, like adults, vary widely in how often they defecate. Some youngsters go several times a day while others may excrete twice a week. Frequency depends upon constitution, diet, and fluid intake as well as emotional factors. Constipation in children is not uncommon and is usually minor. If it persists, a physical examination by a pediatrician is advisable. In the absence of disease, the following factors should be considered:

As with urination, voluntary control of defecation is something that is conditioned. As the bowel fills to a certain, critical level, a reflexive urge to excrete occurs. Children who delay going to the bathroom for long periods of time and who do this consistently may weaken the reflex. In other words, the message from the bowel to the brain is blurred. Most of us have experienced having the urge to defecate, have needed to hold back for one reason or another, and have found that the urge passes. If we repeated this regularly, we would find that our rate of defecation would drop.

Excessive use of laxatives or enemas can also weaken the reflex, because reliance upon cathartics causes reduced usage of the anal sphincters and interrupts the normal muscle-nerve-brain response chain.

Parents who are constipated themselves are most likely to have children with this same problem. This may be due to a genetic predisposition or to the fact that the parent communicates a sense of anxiety and discomfort about defecation. The constipated adult may talk about the pain that results from hard stools. This can cause youngsters to become afraid of going to the bathroom. If fear leads to avoidance and stool retention, the probability of chronic constipation is increased.

Children who have been exposed to coercive, punitive, or premature toilet training may also be susceptible to constipation. In some families going to the bathroom becomes a power struggle, with the child digging in his heels and resolving not to let go of his "precious" feces. (They must indeed be precious if everyone is making such a big fuss over giving them up!) In most cases, however, the link between methods of toilet training and constipation has not been demonstrated.

The case of eight-year-old Candace represents a typical example of childhood constipation that was quickly and effectively treated. At the time she came to my office she hadn't defecated in a week and a half. Her parents reported that Candace had never gone to the bathroom more than twice a week. In this regard she was like her mother, who had suffered from frequent constipation for most of her life and who made regular use of laxatives.

The birth of a younger brother a year prior to referral had created a lot of resentment in Candace as it represented the first time her "Star of the Show" status had been threatened. She spoke openly of her resentment toward her brother, specifically of his being a pest.

It became clear that what had started out as a case of constipation had turned into an anxiety-ridden power struggle. Candace's parents, understandably worried about her health, constantly urged her to go to the bathroom. The more they insisted, the more she resisted. When the level of parental frustration grew strong enough, attempts were made to force her into the bathroom. Here parents saw to it that she stayed on the commode and checked for stools in the toilet. The anxiety generated by this routine had led Candace to protest, tearfully, each time she was forced to approach the bathroom. She cried, kicked, tensed up, and behaved in a near-hysterical manner. And she continued to withhold her stools.

There were several factors to consider in this case. First was the strong possibility of a familial tendency toward constipation, or, at least, infrequent stools. Since the mother suffered from hard, painful stools, this could have increased her daughter's fear of going to the bathroom. The fact that Candace was a child who naturally defecated infrequently may have aroused the mother's anxiety since it reminded her of her own problems. Such *overidentification*—blurring the separate identities of parent and child—can lead to an unhealthy preoccupation with a specific area of behavior.

Candace's long history of stool retention also made it probable that she had weakened the conditioned reflex that controlled her anal sphincter muscles. She was less likely to be aware of her body's signals to go to the bathroom. Following a vicious cycle, the more she withheld, the weaker the reflex would become.

Third, as Candace continued to remain constipated, her stools became denser and harder. This meant that defecation was likely to be painful and difficult. Since behavior is affected by its consequences, the pain would constitute negative payoff (punishment) for going to the bathroom and lead to avoidance.

Fourth, the power struggle that had been generated by parental cajoling, nagging, demanding, and scrutiny had led Candace to develop extremely negative associations about the bathroom. Thus she developed a genuine anxiety reaction in which she became tense and afraid when approaching the commode.

Finally, the attention that Candace elicited from her parents due to her stool retention was important since it provided her with positive payoff for not defecating. This became especially valuable to her in view of the competition with her baby brother. It is not uncommon for children to regress temporarily in their toilet habits after the birth of a sibling. The older child observes the attention the baby receives when he wets or soils his diaper and may be extremely aware of how much physical cuddling and caressing the infant receives while being changed. He then reverts back to the good old days in an attempt to regain some of what he perceives is lost love. Parents who attend to the older youngster's emotional needs will see such regression quickly fade away.

The first step of the treatment plan was to minimize Candace's feelings of guilt and shame. She was assured that many children had trouble going to the bathroom, that it was not their fault, but that this was something that could be helped. When asked if she wanted to be helped, she replied that she did.

A discussion of who was in charge of Candace's going to the bathroom then ensued. I emphasized that no one could make her go to the bathroom and that she was the boss in this regard. I instructed her parents to cease urging her to defecate or scrutinizing the toilet for signs of her "output."

Since this girl's reflexes were most likely weakened, I attempted to recondition them. Making use of the fact that most children and adults naturally experience the urge to go to the bathroom within a half hour after breakfast, I suggested to Candace that she sit on the toilet for no more than ten minutes and that she do this about twenty-five minutes after the morning meal. She could take a favorite book with her, or engage in some other pleasurable (and hence counter-anxious) behavior while sitting. I emphasized that she did not have to actually defecate but merely should sit and relax. If she excreted, fine; if not, that was okay too.

In order to reduce the pain and discomfort associated with defecating after a prolonged period of stool retention, Can-

dace's pediatrician and I agreed that it would be helpful for her
to take a small amount of mineral oil that would loosen and
soften the stools. She was also advised to drink plenty of
fluids. Care was taken by the doctor not to prescribe the oil in a
dose that would lead to diarrhea. Just enough was used to
make it more comfortable for her to defecate.

Since a lot of positive payoff had come Candace's way as
a consequence of retaining her stools, this contingency needed
to be reversed. I explained to her that I knew that going to the
bathroom could be a hard job for her. Furthermore, since hard
jobs deserved payment, I thought that she deserved to be paid
for successfully defecating. She, her parents, and I agreed that
she would record a point on a chart each time she defecated
and that five points would be redeemed for a favorite mystery
book. It was emphasized that going to the bathroom was Candace's job and hers alone and that it would be up to her to be in
charge. Her parents were to cease any special attention paid to
her toileting behavior with the exception that they were allowed to express mild approval when she successfully defecated.

After one week, Candace returned with her chart and
proudly showed me the two points she had earned. The following week the pattern of two defecations continued. After that,
she began to go more frequently—four and five times a week.
She experienced no anxiety or fear about going to the
bathroom and was pleased with being in charge of her body.
Her reward system was thinned out gradually, so that first she
received a point for every two defecations, then for three,
four, etc., until she spontaneously announced that she didn't
need to be paid anymore. After three weeks the mineral oil
was discontinued and her system was back on a regular routine. I had a few more sessions with Candace, during which
we discussed her feelings toward her brother and developed
some strategies she could use when he annoyed her.

The attitudes and behaviors that parents model with regard to excretion are important. Overemphasis upon going to the bathroom should be avoided as should an exaggerated connection between toileting and dirt, cleanliness, pleasure, or pain. In addition, parents should ensure that the child has healthy, adaptive ways of receiving attention and that his toilet habits do not become a topic of constant scrutiny and discussion.

Soiling

The child who is physically ready for toilet training but who involuntarily soils his pants is exhibiting a condition known technically as *encopresis*. Most children experience periodic "accidents." Only the youngster who is chronically encopretic can be considered to have a problem. Problematic soiling, more common in boys than in girls, can develop for a number of reasons.

In many cases, soiling results from stool retention to a point where fecal bulk makes it impossible for the youngster to hold back. At first a small quantity of feces may leak out (spotting). This can cause the child to panic at his loss of control. Then, anxiety sets in and the child loses total control of his sphincters.

Children who experience occasional bowel accidents and receive ridicule or other forms of punishment for this may become traumatized about the process of defecation. The build up of negative associations (see Chapter 3), can lead to chronic loss of control. Punishment should never be used for the child who exhibits soiling or any other type of toileting problem. This includes punitive approaches such as making the child walk around in dirty underwear. Having him rinse off his dirty clothes is acceptable if the task is not presented in the context of punishment, but, rather, as a legitimate responsibility.

There is evidence that in some, but not all, cases, chronic soiling is a symptom of psychological disturbance. Some authorities have noted that encopresis is common in orphanages and foundling homes and may be related to separation anxiety. Encopresis also occurred frequently in British children who were removed from their homes and placed in rural foster homes during World War II. Other studies have found encopresis to be related to father-absence and to hostile patterns of family communication. Occasionally, one finds a child who seems to be deliberately soiling in order to express anger or "take revenge" against a member of the family. However, this is quite rare, and parents should always assume that the child who soils does so involuntarily.

Most encopresis occurs in children who have been successfully toilet trained but who subsequently lose the ability to control their bowel movements (Secondary encopresis). The most common age range in which this takes place is five to seven years, indicating that the problem may be related to stress associated with school and separation. Less frequently, a child who was never completely toilet trained continues to spot or soil (Primary encopresis). Such youngsters often speak of forgetting to go to the bathroom, or of not feeling the urge to defecate. In contrast with children who have been traumatized, the primary encopretic often shows little or no discomfort about his problem; he may even walk around in soiled clothes for hours. Youngsters exhibiting primary encopresis are also likely to display chronic *daytime* wetting. There is probably a familial or constitutional factor operating in such cases.

Children who soil should receive both a comprehensive physical examination by a pediatrician and a workup by a child psychologist. It is unwise for parents to deal with this problem by themselves. The origins of encopresis are complex. In addition, this particular problem can generate considerable anger on the part of parents, making it hard for them to react dispassionately and objectively. Parents should be familiar, however, with the various treatment approaches that have been used for encopresis.

Children whose soiling stems from stool retention—and these constitute the majority of encopretics—can be helped by approaches similar to those previously described in the section on constipation. The child is encouraged to assume responsibility for going to the bathroom. He is assured that he is not alone in his problem and that other children have the same difficulty. Often this will amaze the child and he will be noticeably relieved, as if an enormous burden has been lifted from his chest. The guilt and shame that youngsters experience over problems of toileting cannot be overemphasized.

His parents are asked not to urge or nag him to go to the bathroom—although children aged 4 or 5 may require some initial, low-key parental prompting. The child is further instructed to sit on the toilet at a regularly scheduled time—twenty to thirty minutes after breakfast is especially good because it coincides with a natural urge to defecate—but not to worry about defecating. He is allowed to engage in pleasurable activities while on the commode. Successful defecation into the toilet is rewarded. If prolonged withholding has led to impacted feces, the pediatrician may need to remove these either chemically or mechanically before the onset of treatment. Initially, mineral oil may be used to soften the stools—but only in small doses. It is important to avoid softening the stools to such an extent that the child cannot gain muscular control. For children who do not defecate during the after-breakfast period, sitting on the commode at other times of the day can be suggested. Some doctors have advised having the child sit on the toilet for brief periods three or four times a day. The object of this approach is to encourage regular excretion and avoid excessive buildup of fecal matter.

Youngsters whose soiling is not associated with stool retention can also benefit from a reward system. In such cases, positive payoff is offered for periods of cleanliness rather than for defecating in the toilet. Thus, the child may receive a reward following each day he does not soil. Such an approach has been successful both for children who have never been toilet trained and those who have lost control due to anxiety. The fact that rewarding the child often brings about cessation of soiling should not be taken to imply that encopresis is voluntary. The reward may serve as an incentive that helps override the effects of anxiety.

In cases where a child's soiling is tied in with other psychological problems, individual and family psychotherapy may be useful. Even in such cases, however, it will usually be advisable to work directly upon helping the child learn appropriate bowel control. There are doctors who see encopresis as a symptom of underlying psychopathology and who may be reluctant to work directly upon "the symptom." They may claim that the key is to help the child uncover his conflicts and achieve insight. Unfortunately, insight does not magically lead to successful sphincter control in a child who has not learned to master the feelings and behaviors associated with defecation. In fact, *encopresis can be a source of psychological problems* in that it causes other children to avoid the youngster, call him "Stinky," and leads to social isolation. Ethical considerations dictate, therefore, that direct dealing with the soiling not be unduly postponed.

I have emphasized the importance of not punishing the child suffering from enuresis, chronic constipation, or soiling. There will be instances, however, when the youngster's problem causes him to miss out on pleasurable activities. For example, one of my patients consistently soiled in the swimming pool, causing considerable discomfort to the members of his family. I advised his parents to restrict his use of the pool until he could demonstrate more control. Specifically, he was allowed to swim only on days following a twenty-four hour "clean" period; soiling would lead to immediate removal from the pool for the remainder of the day. Swimming proved to be a potent reward for this boy; the incentive to swim accelerated his bowel control. Similarly, youngsters who soil in public places, such as concert halls and movie theaters, may have to be excluded from these experiences until their control is increased.

A reward approach has also been used successfully for children who soil due to an organic disease. Dr. Robert Kohlenberg of the University of Washington reported the case of a thirteen-year-old boy who had a section of his colon removed surgically due to a condition known as Hirschprung's Disease and who had never been toilet trained. A physical examination revealed that this youngster had inadequate muscle tone in his anal sphincter. Dr. Kohlenberg inserted a fluid-filled balloon in the boy's rectum. The balloon was attached to a fluid-filled tube. The level of fluid in the tube rose as pressure was exerted on the balloon. In this way, Dr. Kohlenberg was able to measure miniscule amounts of muscle tone. By rewarding the boy with money for gradually increasing degrees of pressure, he was able to significantly increase this youngster's sphincter strength. Eventually, the boy was able to control his bowels. Similar work has been done by Dr. Karen Olness at the University of Minnesota. These treatment approaches are exciting because they offer hope to children previously thought of as permanently incontinent.

12

Compulsive Habits

Ritual and repetition are major components of childhood. There is an intrinsic compulsiveness in many of the ways with which children deal with their environment. Several of the most durable and popular games of childhood incorporate compulsive repetition of actions or phrases. In Hopscotch and Jumprope, for example, repeated physical activity is accompanied by the chanting of rhymes. In Simon Says and Red Light-Green Light, movement is not allowed until the child seeks permission in conformance with a rigidly defined verbal code.

Childhood rituals also occur when youngsters carefully avoid stepping on cracks in the sidewalk, insist upon touching every single post on a picket fence, refuse to go to sleep until a detailed check of the closet has been made, or meticulously remove all the A's and M's out of a bowl of alphabet soup before agreeing to eat.

A certain degree of compulsiveness and ritual enters into the various collections to which certain children devote so much of their time. It is not unusual for a single child to amass—at the same time—boxes of baseball cards, bottle caps, comic books, and postage stamps. Parents are often amazed at how conscientious the child can be—cataloguing, arranging, counting, and recording his treasures—while displaying no effort toward keeping his room clean.

The emotional security that comes from structure is probably the major reason behind the tendency for children to construct so many rituals for themselves. The child is not equipped, nor is he allowed, to exert total control over his own life. However, he is able to find comfort from the fact that a certain game is always played in a certain way. Because children deal most comfortably with tangible *things* rather than abstract *ideas* and concepts, they need visible reminders of security. Some structure is provided by adults in the form of rules and regulations. However, the strictest prohibitions are those which youngsters impose upon themselves.

The ritualistic, almost religious, nature of childrens' games ensures that these activities will endure over time and will remain relatively constant across geographical regions. There is remarkable similarity between the way Hopscotch is played in Maine and the way it is played in California. This can ease communication between children. For example, two youngsters from different cities may find that they have little in common other than a shared knowledge of how to play a certain game. The game thus provides a means of social introduction, and familiarity with its rules serves as a membership card into the International Childrens Club.

Children go through stages during which they become more stereotyped in their behavior than usual. This can happen during periods of stress as the child seeks to compensate for a lack of internal security by increasing the structure of his external world. Peer pressure also plays a major role in the development of rituals, for as youngsters enter new social groups they quickly assume the ritualistic behavior of their cohorts. For the most part it is best to ignore minor increases in compulsive or ritualistic behavior, other than to check for undue stress in the child's life.

Obsessions and Compulsions

There will be times when the intensity of ritualistic behavior can disrupt the child's daily life. In such instances there is usually a great deal of anxiety; the youngster feels unable to control his thoughts and actions. Such problematic rituals are generally classified as obsessive-compulsive disorders and require professional psychological treatment.

Obsessions are persistent thoughts which intrude upon the child's train of thought and refuse to go away. *Compulsions* are similarly uncontrollable behaviors. At times obsessive thoughts occur by themselves; on other occasions they are paired with compulsive behavior. Some of the more common obsessive-compulsive childhood problems relate to fear of disease and contamination. Nagging worries about dirt can lead to handwashing and other cleaning compulsions. These episodes may follow a particularly unpleasant illness or may develop in a child whose family is overly preoccupied with health and illness. Obsessive concerns about not doing things exactly right can cause a child to prolong a simple act and delay its completion for an unreasonable length of time. For example, the child may interrupt dressing himself repeatedly in order to make sure that every button is in place and every article of clothing is just so. The simple act of putting on clothes becomes an hour-long production. Some youngsters harbor obsessive doubts that cause them to check and double check any answer to their questions. Persistent fears of causing harm to others may bring about extreme guilt. Tics and twitches represent compulsive behaviors that are translated into repeititive motor movement.

There is no clearcut answer as to why certain children develop obsessive-compulsive problems. Early theories stressed psychological trauma during that period of development when toilet skills are learned. However, subsequent research has failed to establish a connection between toilet-training and obsessiveness. Most doctors who have worked with obsessive-compulsive children have noted that these youngsters tend to be well-behaved, quiet, and somewhat perfectionistic. They may engage in more than one type of compulsive ritual. A visit to a child's home may reveal shoes lined up in a closet with the toes placed precisely at a certain angle. Obsessiveness does not imply uniform neatness, however, and a child can be extremely meticulous about one type of behavior while remaining totally unconcerned about other areas of functioning. There is a definite tendency for compulsive children to have at least one parent who exhibits the same type of behavior. It has been suggested that parents of obsessive-compulsive children set unusually high standards of behavior for themselves and their children, rewarding extreme degrees of orderliness.

Anxiety is a prime ingredient of obsessions and compulsions. In fact, compulsive behavior can be regarded as an attempt to relieve the anxiety generated by obsessive thoughts. The youngster who cannot stop thinking about becoming ill may attempt to engage in symbolic behaviors such as handwashing that temporarily relieve his worries. In this way compulsions can be regarded as a special type of *superstitious* behavior. A specific act (handwashing) becomes associated with short-term reduction of anxiety even though realistically it has nothing to do with preventing illness. Of course, obsessions and compulsions are not unique to children. One of the most famous examples in literature involves Lady Macbeth's compulsive handwashing as she attempts to relieve her guilt about participating in murder. Similarly, Charles Dickens's attorney Jaggers in *A Tale of Two Cities* is a compulsive handwasher.

Though the compulsive act begins as a way of reducing anxiety, it quickly becomes a problem in itself. The child quickly finds out that he is not able either to stop washing his hands or cease worrying about his health. The essential psychological distress in obsessive-compulsive disorders is *anxiety over loss of control.* Children who engage in obsessive-compulsive behavior usually are extremely upset about their inability to stop the behavior. They may regard themselves as weak and incompetent and can become extremely depressed as a result.

It is not helpful to keep reminding the child of his compulsive behavior, for this creates more anxiety and further loss of control. It is hard for parents to disengage themselves from the child's activities because compulsions can be very annoying and disruptive to the family. Care should be exercised so that the child's problem does not bring about major change in the family pattern. For example, the child who prolongs the process of dressing himself for an hour before a family outing, should not be nagged nor should he be allowed to keep everyone else waiting. Rather, he should be informed that the car will leave at a certain time *with or without him.* In situations where he must go along, he should be gently but firmly guided into the car no matter what his state of dress or undress. This should not be done in a punitive manner but should be part of the family's attempt at maintaining behavioral normalcy when presented with a specific habit problem.

Psychological treatment of obsessive-compulsive disorders is difficult. However, notable success has been achieved utilizing a reward approach. The case of Josh illustrates how such a technique can be used.

Josh, an intelligent, well-behaved eleven-year-old boy

was referred to me because of a long history of compulsive nose wiping. This behavior began during a severe case of the flu during which Josh did have a runny nose and needed to wipe it. His behavior persisted, however, after he had become well; it increased to the point where the skin above his mouth had become red and raw. Josh's parents had asked him to stop and had resorted to scolding, all to no avail. Like many children with compulsive tendencies, Josh was a good student and rather quiet. He rarely expressed his feelings and preferred to spend time by himself. He also exhibited other compulsive habits such as arranging his clothes in the closet with the hangers pointing all in the same direction, and was a great worrier. Josh's father described himself as compulsive and perfectionistic and blamed himself for being too hard on his son.

After speaking with Josh, I could see that he was very upset about not being able to stop wiping his nose. When I told him it was possible to control this behavior, he perked up noticeably. I asked him to record each time he wiped his nose for one week and to bring in these records the next time he came to see me. This he did and it was clear that the rate of nose wiping was extremely high, ocurring mostly in the late afternoon after school.

I asked Josh how long he felt he could go without wiping his nose. He thought for a while and said that he could probably last twenty minutes. I then told him that I knew not wiping for such a long time was hard work and that I felt he should be paid for it. After discussion with Josh and his parents, it was decided that he would set aside a twenty-minite period at the beginning of each hour from three to eight P.M. during which he would try not to wipe his nose. For each twenty-minute block of time during which he was successful, he would receive a quarter. He was to keep written records of his progress.

The following week Josh's chart showed that he had gone

for twenty-minute periods several times each afternoon without wiping his nose. I praised him for his self-control and asked him if he was now ready to go for an hour without wiping. He said that he was and it was agreed that he would receive a quarter for each hour during which no nose wiping took place. His success that week varied from two to five hours each night with a clear pattern of increasing control. The goal for success was increased each week with Josh's approval, so that by the end of five weeks he was able to go for a full day (fifteen hours) without wiping his nose. He was extremely proud of his success, and I emphasized that he had mastered his problem himself and would continue to feel more and more control over his body. Not long after, he announced that nose wiping was no longer a problem and that he no longer wished to be paid for abstaining.

I continued to see Josh for psychotherapy because there were other issues that needed to be dealt with. However the removal of an annoying compulsive habit proved very rewarding for him and increased his sense of self-worth and competence.

This approach, in which the child is *rewarded for not engaging in compulsive behavior*, attempts to counteract a previous pattern of learning. The compulsive child associates his habit with the initial reduction of anxiety. In this way compulsions provide positive payoff. In order to override this benefit, incentive is provided not to engage in the old, familiar routine. Establishing initial goals that the child can easily master provides early success that helps fight feelings of being out of control.

A similar treatment approach has been used for muscular tics by a colleague of mine at Childrens Hospital of Los Angeles, Dr. James Varni. While working at Johns Hopkins Medical School, Dr. Varni treated a seven-year-old boy who had four separate compulsive tics: Facial grimaces, shoulder shrugs, rump protusion, and saying "huh." Dr. Varni and his colleagues had the boy sit in front of a mirror so that he could observe his motor habits. He was then rewarded if he could go five minutes without exhibiting more than ten tics by being allowed to play. The boy was given a large stopwatch that allowed him to time the five-minute periods. The criterion for success was gradually increased until the boy was expected to exhibit no tics at all in order to earn his reward (in this case, being allowed to play). The child's mother was taught how to carry out this program at home. Within several weeks all of the tics were eliminated.

"Forbidden" Thoughts

Children harbor secret thoughts that they may regard as sinful, evil, or forbidden. Hostile feelings toward loved ones are normal in children of all ages. Most common are wishes that something unpleasant will befall a brother, sister, or parent. Children may go so far as to wish another member of the family seriously injured or dead. These fantasies are short-lived and, unless they become translated into dangerous behavior, are not cause for alarm.

Problems do arise when a child's secret wishes cause him to experience an inordinate amount of guilt. Burdened with shame, the youngster may try to relieve his anxiety by stopping the thoughts. However, due to his heightened fear and loss of control, the more he tries to suppress them, the stronger they become. This can occur in a child who is not accustomed to expressing his feelings verbally and whose family background emphasizes guilt, shame, and retribution. Religious doctrines that do not differentiate between evil thoughts and evil deeds are also likely to elicit extreme guilt. Once special emphasis has been placed upon control it is difficult deliberately to suppress a thought. For example. someone who is told, *"Don't think of zebras, no matter what!"* generally experiences even more persistent images of white and black striped animals. While thoughts of zebras might be harmless, recurrent ''forbidden'' thoughts can lead to deep shame and self-loathing. The child may come to identify himself with the evil thoughts so that he views himself as a bad person. The understandable result is loss of self-esteem, depression, and withdrawal.

Youngsters who confess to harboring forbidden thoughts should be informed that many children have such thoughts from time to time. The parent who suspects that the child has a good deal of suppressed anger or hostility can encourage open expression either through talking or nonverbal means such as drawing. Once the child recognizes his behavior as normal, his anxiety is likely to drop and the disturbing thoughts will become less intrusive. In instances where persistent unpleasant thoughts linger, it is best to seek psychological help. Such was the case with Ralph.

Ralph, a pleasant twelve-year-old boy had recurrent ''bad feelings.'' While he would not describe these feelings to his parents in any detail, it was clear that they caused him a great deal of distress. Indeed, Ralph had spoken of wanting to kill himself.

During our first session together, Ralph let me know that he often thought of burning his house down and killing his mother. He was tormented by these obsessions. ''Why would I feel that way about Mom? I love her more than anyone!'' he asked. Ralph was not a psychotic child, nor was he seriously disturbed. He functioned well in school, had lots of friends, and in general got along with his parents. There was a slight degree of emotional struggle between him and his father but no more than could be expected in many families. There was no likelihood that he would act upon his thoughts.

What alarmed me was that the recurrent thoughts had caused Ralph's self-esteem to plummet. Things had gotten to the point where he referred to himself as a bad person and talked of committing suicide. Clearly quick action was called for.

First I explained to Ralph that his "feelings" were not mysterious and that they were thoughts. In as authoritative a tone as I could muster, I told him that such thoughts were normal and that many children had them. I emphasized the distinction between thinking and doing. Initially Ralph reacted with doubt, then he brightened. I said that he was having so much trouble stopping the thoughts because he was afraid of them; what was really bothering him was not being able to control himself. He nodded his head vigorously and replied that that was exactly true—his helpflessness made him feel weird and bad.

The therapeutic goal then became clear. Ralph would need to learn to associate unpleasant thoughts with a sense of control, so that the former anxiety-rovoking association would be eliminated. In order to accomplish this, I had him practice having the thoughts in my office. This changed the context of the obsessions from threatening, forbidden evil impulses to merely another type of thought. The fact that I instructed him to have the thoughts let him know that I was sincere about their being normal.

Then, I had Ralph practice having the thoughts and making them go away by visualizing a red stop sign and telling himself the word *Stop*. Following this he saw himself engaged in a favorite activity—playing baseball. This behavioral technique—*thought-stopping*—is very effective in the treatment of obsessions, and the key to its success is in replacing a negative mental image with a harmless one. The mind cannot remain empty. For this reason, merely trying to make a thought go away is difficult. (Remember those zebras!) However if the person is able to substitute one thought for another, he fills up mental space and gains more control. Telling a person to

"Stop thinking about zebras" is less helpful than is an instruction to "stop thinking about zebras and think about giraffes."

Ralph alternated having the unpleasant thoughts and seeing the stop sign until he became quite proficient. He was instructed to go home, have at least ten bad thoughts a day, and make as many of them as possible go away using the stop sign. I said that if he wanted to have more than ten thoughts that would be all right with me, but ten was a bare minimum. He was to keep written records of his thoughts and to note how successful he had been in stopping them.

At our next meeting Ralph announced somewhat sheepishly that he had only been able to have nine bad thoughts. I sighed and feigned disappointment, which made both of us laugh, and then I told him that he had better come through with at least seven or eight thoughts the following week. Needless to say, he found himself unable to do this more than twice and reported an inability to come up with more than four or five bad thoughts. More important than the reduction in the frequency of obsessions was the change in Ralph's emotional reaction to them. In the past the recurrent thoughts had caused him a great deal of shame; now he seemed quite casual about them and began to see himself as the competent, masterful young man that he truly was.

Within a few more weeks the disturbing thoughts disappeared completely. I continued to counsel Ralph and his parents regarding other family issues and have maintained active contact with him. He is happy, well-adjusted, and feels that he will be able to handle disturbing thoughts if they come up in the future.

13

A Death in the Family

Until recently, the subject of death and dying was avoided in open discussion. This was especially true with regard to children, who were considered too inexperienced and vulnerable to be able to handle death-related information. It was thought that children could not really grasp the concept of death. Within the last decade, however, there has been a reversal of these attitudes, and a new academic field—thanatology, the study of death—has emerged. One positive result has been a wealth of research data on children and death.

It is now clear that children begin at an early age to develop an understanding of death. Their perceptions differ from those of adults and change constantly as they grow and mature. But death is of real concern to most youngsters and children profit from an open approach that allows them to ask questions, takes into account their psychological development, and helps them to express their feelings.

The child under two reacts with anxiety to separation and abandonment, but he does not have a clearcut idea of death as a special event. Children this young, with the exception of the most precocious, are unlikely to profit from specific explanations regarding death. They will of course need reassurance, comfort, and support upon losing a loved person or animal.

Children develop a rudimentary concept of death at about the age of three (with variations accounting for individual differences). Between the ages of three and six, the child's primary concern will continue to be separation, but he will gradually comprehend that death is somewhat different from other forms of separation. He will observe that insects and animals die. He may see death portrayed on television or in the movies and can observe the reactions of people close to him. As he approaches school age, he may come across mentions or descriptions of death on the printed pages.

The notion that death is an event that happens to other people (but not to him) is something that will emerge in the child from three to five. Separation fears may become more intense; the focus is on the threat of loss—as opposed to fears of his own death. He may worry about being abandoned, left alone, or his anxiety may take the form of sleep disturbances such as nightmares and insomnia. Some children may react by clinging to their parents or showing increased dependence in other ways.

Preschool children often become preoccupied with the "nuts and bolts" of dying—the biological details. Parents may be distressed at the matter-of-fact way in which a young child receives the news of the death of a relative. However, if we realize that preschool children do not generally see death as irreversible and fully expect the departed to return, their casual reactions can be understood. A child may say, "Dead people can taste, but they can't hear," or, "Some dead people like to eat, others don't"; these concepts that seem bizarre to us are comprehensible when we are aware of the temporary way in which children view dying. Despite patient parental explanations, apparent understanding on Monday may give way on Tuesday to the same "illogical" questions and statements.

Young children are likely to make superstitious associations regarding death. For example, if they are told that someone died in a specific house, they may view the house as being in some way responsible for causing death. An avoidance of the house is likely to follow. This is due both to the youngsters' incomplete understanding of causality and to the childhood tendency to *generalize*.

Children above the age of six begin *gradually* to expand their understanding of death in several ways. They begin to comprehend that death is irreversible; dead people do not return to life. They also start to realize that death is inevitable; it happens to all living creatures, and dying is something that can happen to them. Coming to grips with such information can be extremely threatening. The realization that his body is perishable often causes the primary school age child to develop sudden and extreme concerns about his health. He may ask numerous questions about illness or develop vague aches, pains, and other symptoms for which no medical cause can be found. This apparent hypochondriasis is a normal reaction to the frightening insights he has begun to acquire regarding his own mortality.

While anxiety about abandonment can persist into the primary school years, the child's questions about death will take on a new emphasis: He will show a high degree of concern about pain and suffering and the physical sensations associated with dying. He may ask, "Does it hurt to die?" or, "How does Grandpa feel now that he's dead?" He may inquire, "How can you breathe after they bury you and put dirt over your face?"—a question that indicates he is not yet fully aware of death as the ending of bodily processes.

In contrast with the three-, four-, and five-year-old who views death as being left alone, the youngster above the age of six is likely to *personify* death. Mr. Death, the Bogeyman, the Wicked Witch, the Dying Monster, the Angel of Death, and so forth are all vivid representations of death to the primary school youngster. The drawings that he produces at this age can be fantastic and imaginative.

For the six-, seven-, and eight-year-old, death is often seen as someone or something who comes in the night. Children who develop nocturnal anxiety or fear of the dark may be expressing death-related worries.

By the age of eleven, most children have the ability to comprehend that death is irreversible, that it happens to everyone, that it is a physiological process involving the cessation of respiration and other bodily processes, and that he is mortal. The preadolescent will no longer speak of death as a monster, nor will he be preoccupied with abandonment. And he realizes that the deceased is not coming back. In response to the question "What is death?" many nine-, ten-, and eleven-year-olds will answer, "Death is when you stop breathing," or, "A person dies when he stops living and his body stops working." As young people enter the teen years, the focus of their anxiety may shift to philosophical issues such as "Why do people have to die?" or "What is the meaning of life?" or "Is there a possibility of reincarnation?" Teens and pre-teens may discuss these concerns with parents or prefer to talk to those their own age.

Talking to Children About Death: What Not to Say

Dr. Earl Grollman in his excellent book, *Explaining Death to Children*, points out that What Not to Say is often as important, if not more important, as What To Say. Here are a number of approaches that Grollman feels are not helpful to children.

Don't offer the child an explanation that deviates from your own belief. Children are quick to see beyond the content of an adult's words and will often focus on *how* those words are being said. If you don't believe in life ever after, you should not feel the need to reassure your child, by offering him such a picture. Your credibility will be in doubt. Why are Mom or Dad so upset about Grandma's death if they believe that Grandma is going to heaven to dance with angels? The child who senses a discrepancy between what is being told to him and what his parent feels will suspect that something is being withheld. His fantasies about what is being concealed are likely to be more terrifying than the truth of what the parent believes. On the other hand, if you sincerely adhere to certain religious beliefs, these should be communicated. It is advisable to avoid descriptions of death or the hereafter that are ambiguous. Children tend to think concretely and it is not until the pre-teen years that abstract (symbolic) reasoning begins to dominate their thinking. The seven-year-old sees Santa Claus as a real person who actually comes down the chimney rather than as a historical figure who symbolizes Christmas. Similarly, the Angel of Death may have metaphorical meaning for adults but the child will view him as an actual creature, and quite a frightening one.

Don't refer to death as sleep or as a journey. As had been mentioned, identification of death with sleep can cause the child to develop anxiety about the dark. He may be afraid to go to sleep for fear he may never wake up or even be afraid of closing his eyes. If a child hears that the deceased "went away on a long trip," he will be led to expect a return from that trip. In younger children this plays upon an already incompletely developed sense of the finality of death and will lead to chronic anxiety and constant questions such as "When is Grandma coming back?" Worries like these increase over time, and at some point it will be necessary to explain that the dead person will not come back. If this follows an initial, inaccurate explanation, the child will be confused about the contradiction and may feel betrayed and insecure about what to believe. It is crucial to be honest.

Don't equate death with a reward for being good. Many adults feel they are helping the child by saying something like "God took Grandma to be with Him because she was so good." Dr. Grollman points out that the good may indeed die young, but there are many fine people who live to a ripe old age. There is no organized religion that stresses untimely death as a reward. The child can sense that death brings sadness. Why should people be sad, he asks himself, if the dead person is being rewarded? He may even feel that *he* will be "rewarded" with death if he is too good.

Don't present death as a form of punishment. Children are likely to make exaggerated connections between their actions and external events. The youngster who sees death as retribution may grow apprehensive about *any* action for fear that his behavior will bring about the ultimate punishment. Children have a natural tendency to assume guilt and do not profit from messages that intensify such feelings.

What to Say

Often the most valuable support you can offer your child when a death occurs in the family is through nonverbal communication. Holding and touching the child reassures him and lets him know that he is loved. Aside from this, it is important to understand what your child is really asking when he inquires about death and to tailor your answers to the child's development level. A question such as "Why did Grandpa go away?" may be a straightforward request for information. More often, however, the child is seeking comfort and reassurance. Unless he persists in repeated and specific questions, it is best to avoid detailed answers that dwell upon the philosophical meaning of death. Offer an answer such as: "Grandpa died. I don't really know why, but it wasn't because of anything anybody did. I miss him a lot and I know you do too. But don't worry, because I'm not going to leave you, and I'll be here to take care of you."

What children need during bereavement is an emphasis on life—the value and quality of their own lives and the lives of those important to them. It is helpful to emphasize the positive aspects of the deceased. Let the child know that although Grandpa is gone, he is remembered by loved ones. Talk about the accomplishments and unique qualities of the deceased and allow the child to contribute his remembrances.

Young children may ask direct questions such as "Are you going to die, Mommy?" and may repeat the same questions many times as they attempt to assimilate stressful information. Try to be patient and offer repeated, consistent explanations, assuring the child that you will be with him and able to care for him.

Don't be dismayed if the young child makes remarks that seem insensitive or macabre. His curiosity about how organs cease functioning, the process of decay, and other biological phenomena are all necessary for a concrete "picture" of death and do not reflect insensitivity. Answer questions simply and factually.

Children who feel somehow guilty or responsible for a death should be quickly reassured that they have no cause for these feelings. They may need to be reassured about contagion fears—informed that what caused the death of another person will not cause them to die. This kind of information will be most relevant for primary school age youngsters, who have a growing awareness of their bodies. They will also benefit from being told explicitly that the deceased is not suffering.

Children, even those young children who may not be able to fully comprehend the meaning of this, should be told that death is irreversible. It is possible to be honest yet supportive if factual explanations are accompanied by gestures of comfort. Simple statements such as ''People who die don't come back'' or ''Grandpa won't be with us anymore because he died'' often serve as stimuli for further discussion.

Preadolescent youngsters will begin to entertain ''adult'' concerns about death, and parents may be at a loss to answer their more sophisticated questions. Why do people have to die? Why do some people die at an old age and others before their time? What happens to people after they die—do their thoughts continue, separate from their bodies?

Once again, even when dealing with philosophical issues, it is important to avoid confusing, ambiguous language. It is also perfectly appropriate to say ''I don't know'' when this is the truthful answer. While children may be initially surprised to realize that their parents are not omniscient, this is a valuable learning experience.

Even the highly verbal pre-teen who offers a barrage of philosophical inquiries will benefit from receiving emotional support. Often what he is really saying is ''I want comfort. I want to know that I'll be okay.''

If you believe in life after death, transmit these ideas to your child. If you feel that life ceases with death, don't be afraid that your views are too harsh for your child to tolerate. Talk with him about the beauty of life, stressing the importance of living each day to its fullest.

Death of a Pet

When a favorite household animal dies an opportunity exists for a valuable learning experience. While adults may grieve over the loss of a pet, they are usually less emotionally involved than children. This makes it easier for parents to help the child cope.

The death of a pet should not be taken lightly by grown-ups. When I see new patients, I customarily take a stress history to find out what major changes have occurred in the child's life during the previous year or so. Children often mention the loss of a favorite cat, dog, bird, or other animal as a significant event—sometimes to the surprise of their parents. Feelings of grief can persist for several months after the actual death.

The circumstances of the death of a pet should not be concealed. Nor should well-meaning adults try to replace the lost animal immediately with another one. The child needs time to grieve. If the death of a pet represents his first direct experience with death, important concepts can be communicated in realistic, age-appropriate terms. He can begin to learn that death is irreversible by hearing that his dog is gone and will not come back. The lack of connection between death and punishment can be stressed as the child is reassured that losing Champ or Missy was not his fault.

Children frequently want to engage in elaborate funeral rituals for pets. These can include a eulogy, a "service," and burial or cremation. Such ceremonies should be encouraged. Participating in a funeral for a pet provides the child with the chance to actively "work through" his feelings of loss. By taking part in the rituals, he is comforted by structure and routine, feels useful, and can express his emotions about the beloved animal. By witnessing the burial or cremation he gains a sense of closure—of finality and completeness—about the loss. All of this helps in attaining a sense of control during a stressful time.

Death of a Loved One

The death of a grandparent or other older adult is the first human loss that children are likely to encounter. The child's reaction will depend not only upon his age and experience, but also upon his relationship with the dead person. If Grandma or Grandpa was remote, he may appear relatively unmoved by the death. If, on the other hand, a close emotional bond existed, the response is likely to be more agitated.

The child will imitate the grieving behaviors of the adults around him. Parents may find it very difficult to mourn the loss of their own parent and at the same time comfort a youngster. They may worry about crying or showing sadness in front of the child and feel they should be strong and stoic. Such concerns, though well-intended, are usually unwarranted. It is appropriate for parents and children to cry and be sad together. *Grieving and mourning are normal therapeutic processes.* Though painful, such behaviors help people to express feelings of loss and receive comfort from others.

Children who are excluded from the mourning process can feel alienated from the family. Lacking accurate information, they are likely to develop fantasies that are more frightening than the truth, are often guilt-producing, and can generate a host of anxious symptoms. Psychological research has also made it clear that suppression of initial feelings of grief can lead to emotional difficulties some time after the death.

Parents whose own level of grief keeps them from spending an extended time with their children should be allowed the privacy they require. In such cases the child can be told that Dad or Mom needs time alone because he or she is feeling very sad but that this is not due to anything the child has done. The care of the child can be entrusted to the other parent or to a relative or close friend. In any case, the responsible adult should be aware of the need to integrate the child into the mourning experience.

Children need to have their feelings *validated,* to be told that what they are feeling during times of stress is normal and okay. Such feelings can include confusion, fear, sadness, and anger. Anger often takes the form of hostility toward the dead person, and in this, young children can be especially uninhibited. If a child says, "I'm mad at Grandpa for dying" or, "If Grandma would have loved me she wouldn't have left me," a reprimand is not helpful.

Young children are typically preoccupied with themselves to an extreme degree. They see themselves as the center of the universe and gauge events in terms of how they are personally affected. Open hostility toward a dead person is a healthy, normal reaction. If not suppressed, it will be temporary. If hostility is unexpressed, the child may internalize his feelings and feel extremely guilty.

Hostility can also be *displaced*—expressed not toward the dead person but toward someone else. The grieving child may become angry at even the most sensitive, caring person because that person isn't Grandma. On the other hand, feelings of *attachment* can also be displaced so that sudden, strong dependency upon a new person takes place. Often the object of these transferred affections is someone the child identifies with the deceased.

In helping children express feelings about death, both verbal and nonverbal pathways should be explored. Children may want to talk about their sadness and anger, or they may communicate through play, sculpture, and drawing. Adequate play materials should be provided so that this can take place. Don't be surprised if the child produces angry, confused pieces of artwork or if his games seem violent or morbid. Impromptu games "invented" during this period may include reconstructing the death. Through observing these activities, attentive adults receive clues as to the youngster's perception of what has happened; they can thereby correct possible misconceptions.

Don't pressure a child to talk about his feelings. The most helpful message to offer him is: "It's okay to talk and it's okay not to talk. If you feel like talking I'll be here to listen to you." One way of facilitating communication is to talk about your own feelings. After hearing Mom, Dad, or another important adult say, "This is a hard time for me. Sometimes I feel sad or just plain mixed up." the child may find it easier to express his confusion. He will feel less embarrassed about saying or thinking "silly" things.

Most children above the age of seven should be *encouraged*—but not pressured—to attend the funeral of a loved one. As we have noted, funerals are formalized, concrete ways of saying good-bye. Youngsters benefit from active participation in the farewell process and, if excluded, often feel unworthy or undeserving.

The child who attends a funeral for the first time will be apprehensive. Prepare him beforehand by explaining what will happen and how he might feel and offer a good deal of physical comfort. Preparation for funerals is not unlike preparation for other stressful experiences. A parent might say, "Grandpa's body will be placed in a box called a coffin. The minister is going to say a prayer, and then the coffin will be lowered into the ground and covered with dirt. You may see people crying and you may find yourself feeling sad or afraid or just plain strange. If you want to cry, that's okay and if you don't, that's okay too. I'll be here with you." Inquiries about what the coffin looks like inside or how the dead person can breathe with dirt over his face should be answered factually. The same principle applies to questions about cremation.

If a child is exceptionally high strung it may be best for him not to attend the funeral, so long as he is left with a knowledgeable, supportive adult. Youngsters who resist attending funerals even after being given accurate descriptive information should have their wishes honored.

While the loss of a grandparent can be explained as an inevitable occurrence in the life span, the death of a younger person will be more traumatic for everyone. The death of a parent can be staggering for a child, and the death of a sibling can be particularly threatening in terms of survivor guilt or extreme contagion fears. The death of a classmate is also likely to evoke substantial contagion fears. It is my strong feeling that youngsters experiencing the loss of a parent or sibling can benefit greatly from short-term psychological counseling. In the case of the loss of a classmate, counseling might take place in a group setting—for example, in the school itself.

As much as is possible, parents should avoid making comparisons between the living child and his dead brother or sister. Similarly, the practice of setting a child up as a replacement for a dead adult is distinctly harmful. Telling a youngster ''Now that Daddy's gone you're going to have to take care of your mother'' or ''Now it's going to be important for you to be a strong Little Man'' places him in a position of responsibility for which he is psychologically and physically not equipped. A seven-year-old does not magically assume the capabilities of an adult. Exhortations to remain strong also lead children to suppress their emotions and prevent them from appropriately expressing their feelings. Some children may seem to embrace the adult role with relish, transforming themselves into minature men and women. Such hyper-maturity often results in a caricature of adult behavior and can lead to serious psychological problems later in life. Individuals who have been forced into an unnatural role during childhood often carry a tremendous rage that becomes translated into self-destructive behavior in adulthood. *All children have a right to experience the dependency and innocence of childhood.*

Extended Mourning

There are many right ways to grieve. There are no precise criteria for pathological mourning, and there is no arbitrary cut-off point at which a child or adult should be expected to stop grieving and "pull himself together." However, children who are excluded from initial participation in the mourning process may exhibit unusually prolonged reactions. These can lead to psychosomatic reactions, night fears and sleep disturbances, depression, school avoidance, as well as extreme instances of denial in a child who is developmentally able to understand certain death-related concepts. For example, a ten-year-old could be expected to accept the fact that death is irreversible. If, six months after the loss of a loved one, he persists in asking "When is Daddy coming back?" this is an unusual reaction.

Most people who have experienced the death of someone close to them undergo transitory feelings of depression, sadness, and anger for years. However, they are able to resume their normal day-to-day activities within a month or two. The child whose depression prevents him from returning to school or engaging in activities with his peers well after this period may be exhibiting an extreme withdrawal reaction. Such youngsters often persist in making negative statements about themselves such as "I'm no good," "I'm worthless," or "I want to kill myself." They may be listless and uncommunicative or may turn to acting out their distress in destructive physical ways. Prolonged grieving, especially when it results in a major disruption of daily schedules of living, should be handled through professional psychological treatment.

14

Dealing with Disaster

In 1971, a major earthquake struck Southern California, with an epicenter in Sylmar, just outside of Los Angeles. Tremors were felt across a wide geographical area and aftershocks continued for days. The earthquake caused extensive injury and damage to property as well as several deaths. It proved traumatic for both adults and children.

The aftermath of the quake provided a unique opportunity to investigate the psychological effects of disasters and, more important, to provide crisis intervention services to the victims. The San Fernando Valley Child Guidance Clinic of Van Nuys, California, rose to this challenge. Under the direction of Dr. Herbert Balufarb, the clinic volunteered to answer questions about emotional effects of the earthquake upon children and to set up a telephone hot-line to handle communications.

Over eight hundred phone calls came in from concerned parents. The most frequently cited problems were disruptions of children's eating and sleeping pattern. Hot-line counselors advised parents to initiate numerous counter-anxious activities for their children. Bedtime stories, special occasions for drinking hot chocolate or enjoying favorite foods, using a night light, and, most important, frequent reassurance about their safety were among the suggestions. The majority of children quickly returned to normal.

Families who desired more extensive counseling were invited to attend group discussion sessions at the clinic. Three hundred families were counseled over a five-week period, with most parents and children attending only one session. The children in this sample were from three to twelve years old. The most commonly reported stress reactions were fear of sleeping in their own rooms and separation anxiety. This regressive behavior had developed because it helped the children to obtain the extra emotional support necessary during crisis. The parents were assured that temporary regression was normal but cautioned not to allow the behavior to become chronic. They were advised to return children to normal activities such as school and household chores within a few days.

Fearful children were treated in groups and were encouraged to share their experiences with others who had gone through the same trauma. Youngsters who were not able to engage in detailed discussion were helped to draw and play out their feelings.

In 1975, scientists investigated another disaster. A tornado caused extensive damage to Omaha, Nebraska, and surrounding areas. Children experienced insomnia, restless sleep, increased clinging and dependency, fear of storms, clouds, winds, and loud noises. Some youngsters indicated a sense of guilt, saying things such as ''I turned on the tornado.'' Out of forty-six children studied, twenty-six were referred for further mental health consultation. Children with a prior history of psychological problems or family stress were most anxious.

Young tornado victims were encouraged to return to school as soon as possible and no academic problems occurred.

The Nebraska researchers found that honest, scientific explanations of the tornado were best. It was not therapeutic to shield the children from reality, to deny what had happened, or to create stories laced with fantasy. A Tornado Comic Book was used to educate youngsters and to prepare them for future tornadoes in that storm-prone region.

The Omaha team found that anxiety was less severe when families were kept together. For a child, the most traumatic aspect of a disaster can be separation from those upon whom he depends. Telling children that their feelings of anxiety were normal was extremely constructive. The Nebraska children also profited from being allowed to express their feelings verbally and nonverbally. "Playing Tornado" gave them solace.

Children were encouraged to participate in the cleanup of the debris created by the tornado. This helped overcome feelings of helplessness by giving them a structured social role that made them feel useful.

Temporary regression lasted only for a few days in children whose parents maintained normal standards of discipline. The more quickly the home environment returned to normal the sooner the youngster's behavior bounced back to normal.

A third major investigation took place in Granville, Australia, where in 1977, a railway wreck caused extensive loss of lives. Dr. Beverly Raphael of the University of Sydney participated in the psychological first aid of wreck victims and reported upon the effects of this tragedy.

Dr. Raphael raised the important point that the psychological effects of disasters continue after the initial trauma. Furthermore, victims can include not only the survivors and those who mourn the dead but also rescuers, who must maintain emotional and physical strength in the face of tragedy.

For the most part, Dr. Raphael's conclusions were similar to those of the California and Nebraska researchers: Children benefit from open and honest explanations, frequently repeated. Maintenance of family integrity and open expression of feelings are essential. Youngsters whose loved ones have been injured should be encouraged to visit the hospital. Direct contact with unpleasant reality is less destructive than the fantasies created in the minds of children from whom the truth has been "hidden."

Mastering Crisis

If children are to adjust to trauma they must have some understanding of what is going on. Coping with natural disasters is different only in degree from coping with other anxiety-provoking events such as illness and hospitalization. Adults should avoid the impulse to protect the child. On the contrary, active attempts should be made to find out what the youngster understands in order that misconceptions can be corrected.

The following principles can be applied to the aftermath of any traumatic experience when anxiety persists:

Gently Encourage Early Discussions of the Event. You may need to lead the way by talking about your own reactions. If the child "sits on his feelings" don't assume that because he is silent there is nothing on his mind. Children should never be pressured to communicate but must be encouraged to feel comfortable about asking questions. Expression can be verbal or may take the form of drawings or games.

Validate Feelings of Anxiety and Anger. Tell the child that such emotions are normal and acceptable, and will pass.

Provide Accurate Explanations. Correct misconceptions. *especially those that lead to feelings of guilt.* If you cannot answer a particular question, it is appropriate to say "I don't know."

If the Trauma Was Experienced in a Group, Encourage Group Discussion. Listening to others who have gone through the same thing is tremendously reassuring for children. It also gives them the opportunity to model appropriate coping styles.

Provide Counter-Anxious Behaviors. Many of the "enemies of anxiety" discussed in Chapter 3 can be adapted for use in dealing with disasters. Children like to get angry at the earthquake or the storm. They may invent Mr. Tornado or the Flood Monster and delight in drawing him and tearing him up. Other youngsters will play Earthquake and take on the various roles of victims, rescuers, etc. Eating and drinking, also counter-anxious activities, are satisfying in crisis situations.

Accept Temporary Regression but Avoid Chronic Changes in Family Style. Some youngsters will use more babytalk. Others will grow clingy and fearful of being left alone. Sleep disturbances and bad dreams are common reactions. Toilet control may weaken temporarily.

Beyond an initial treat or two, don't provide excessive privileges for the child who is a disaster victim. Given the opportunity to express themselves and receive reassurance, most children will return to usual functioning within a few days.

Use Modeling Constructively. The child who is placed in an unfamiliar situation will be unsure how to act. He will observe the behavior of others for clues as to what reaction is appropriate. Parents who maintain a calm, collected manner and do not panic during crisis influence their children's reactions and attitudes in a positive way.

Minimize Unnecessary Separation or Segregation. During crisis it is often easy to overlook those who have not been hurt. The child who witnesses an accident to his sibling may feel confused and isolated if he is left alone while everyone else goes to the hospital. As an innocent bystander in the tragedy, he will have strong feelings of fear, anger, and sadness that need to be expressed. He will worry about his sister and, like the adults in the family, will want to know about her physical condition. There may be a desire to re-experience the accident in play. The experience of tragedy will not magically disappear just because it is not overtly acknowledged. It is understandable for parents to be engrossed with the problems of an injured child, but they need to reassure their other children as well.

In most cases, natural disasters are unpredictable. However, in many geographical areas a high probability of seasonal floods, tornadoes, monsoons, brushfires, and earthquakes has been historically established. Psychological preparation for possible disaster should be a regular part of civil defense training wherever natural disasters are likely to occur. Applying the principles of emotional expression, guilt reduction, accurate information, and therapeutic modeling can help reduce the psychological fallout for children. In general, this aspect of disaster training has been sorely neglected.

An example of children exposed to a different kind of repetitive trauma occurs in Israel, where shellings and bombings of border settlements are an unfortunate aspect of everyday life. I was visiting a kibbutz near the Jordanian border in 1969 and was present when a terrorist rocket attack caused the air raid siren to sound. Every member of the Kibbutz took refuge in one of several underground security bunkers. I ended up in a bunker full of children, who were being supervised by two day-care workers.

I was impressed by how calmly these youngsters, who ranged in age from three to seven years, reacted to the attack. Of course, they had gone through similar episodes many times before. But their lack of anxiety was undoubtedly due to the way the adults handled the situation.

These Israeli children are prepared for the eventuality of attack as soon as they are old enough to understand what this means. They are told what they are likely to hear and see and are provided with a good many coping mechanisms. For example, the bunker was well-stocked with snacks and soft drinks, and there were a variety of box games and other recreational materials. As the rockets exploded, literally yards away, the Israeli children munched on crackers and played Hebrew versions of Monopoly and Junior Scrabble. They knew what was going on—some of them spoke of the rockets matter-of-factly—but remained composed.

I experienced a degree of sadness at seeing young children so inured to the brutality of war, but given the reality of political tension in that region, it was good to know that chronic anxiety and fear were not inevitable reactions.

Vicarious Exposure to Disaster

In addition to direct experience of disaster, screen or TV portrayals of towering infernos, shark attacks, sinking ships, freeway crashes, exploding dirigibles, and attacks of killer bees can be extremely realistic and frightening to children. While today's child is no more likely than his predecessors to directly experience tragedy, he *is* more likely to hear about or indirectly observe disastrous events. The youngster growing up in the latter part of the twentieth century lives in an age of instant information transfer. A flood in Peru, a ski-lift disaster in Switzerland, or a mass murder in Chicago are brought into his living room within seconds of their occurrence, via the evening news. Both the actual quantity of disaster and vividness of detail to which a contemporary child is exposed are greater than ever. And, as in the case of Mark, such exposure can lead to behavioral symptoms similar to those of disaster victims.

Four-year-old Mark had suddenly begun to show signs of increased anxiety—clinging to his mother and refusing to separate, restless sleep, and constant complaints of being afraid. He had also started to cry for no apparent reason and was reluctant to leave the house to play.

Mark's mother reported that she had taken him to see the movie *Earthquake* in a theater that featured Sensurround— each time an earthquake took place on screen, it was accompanied by intense vibrations that created the illusion of tremor, thus enhancing the realism of the motion picture.

At the beginning of the picture, before the first earthquake took place, Mark announced that he had to go to the bathroom. Since he had previously been able to handle this by himself, his mother let him go alone. As Mark sat on the commode, the first quake hit the screen. The Sensurround vibrations were not confined to the viewing room but were strong enough to rock the lobby and the restrooms. The toilet began to shake violently, with Mark on it. Without warning or preparation he found himself alone in the lavatory stall, holding on for dear life.

There is no way of knowing whether Mark would have been as frightened had he been viewing *Earthquake* in a more conventional manner. It is quite possible that if he had been sitting with his mother, munching on popcorn, and being prepared for what he was going to see on screen, he would not have been unduly anxious. Caught unawares, however, he was traumatized; needless to say, Mark's mother felt guilty about what she "had done to him," even though what had happened had been due entirely to chance.

In treatment, Mark was encouraged to draw what he thought an earthquake looked like. He produced a jumbled, scribbled mass of angry black crayon lines. Then together, he and I built a city using toy blocks. When we finished, we simulated an earthquake and destroyed the city. At first Mark was hesitant to do this but soon he imitated me and was gleefully wreaking havoc upon an entire toy metropolis. He repeated the process of building and destroying several times and was told that he could do the same thing at home, especially if he felt afraid.

I explained to Mark that the earthquake had nothing to do with his going to the bathroom or anything else he had done. I empathized with how frightening it must have been to experience the shaking and told him that most children (or adults) would be afraid after something like that!

Mark's mother was instructed to look out for examples of Mark's assertive, masterful behavior and to praise them. When he said he was afraid, she was to listen sympathetically and suggest he get mad at the earthquake.

Within three weeks all of Mark's anxious symptoms disappeared. He still enjoyed playing earthquake from time to time but could discuss the theater incident without noticeable distress.

Criminal Acts

Criminal acts can be considered in the same category as disasters. As with accidents and natural phenomena such as earthquakes and tornadoes, crime tends to be sudden and traumatic, leaving little time for psychological and physical preparation. This has ramifications not only for the child who has witnessed an attack, robbery, or molestation, but also for the youngster who has been the victim of a crime.

Sexual molestation of children is not an everyday circumstance, but it is by no means rare. In many cases, the molester is someone whom the child knows, even a relative, and the youngster may be reluctant to report the crime. This can be due both to fears of retaliation and to guilt. Children who are molested or attacked often believe that they have somehow played a role in bringing about the event. It is safe to say that sexual crimes against children are grossly underreported.

When a previously healthy outgoing youngster suddenly evidences the behavioral signs of depression and anxiety—loss of appetite, listlessness, slow speech or mutism, nightmares and disordered sleep, fear of being touched, and self-punitive acts—and no medical or psychological reason for this sudden change can be found, parents should consider the possibility that the child has been molested. Immediate professional help should be obtained in such cases.

Children who witness violent acts may develop fears for their own safety as well as survivor guilt. In this sense, the witness should be considered a victim as well, and for him, too, professional consultation is advisable.

15

Finding
Professional Help

When a child suffers from anxiety or fear of complex or unknown origin, parents may not be able to solve the problem without help. In this chapter, we will discuss some specific guidelines for parents to follow and describe briefly the kinds of professionals that might be involved. Needless to say, the more actively parents and children can cooperate with the professionals, the easier it will be to treat emotional difficulties successfully.

Pediatrician

The pediatrician should be the child's *primary health care provider*. He or she serves as the basic source of health care for the child and can direct parents to specialists when necessary. Pediatricians have undergone specialty training in the medical care of children after receiving their M.D. Such training takes the form of an internship and two to three years of residency in pediatrics at an accredited health care facility. The pediatrician passes specialty exams and is then *board certified* in pediatrics. Some doctors then choose to take additional *subspecialty* training in a particular area of pediatrics (pediatric neurology, pediatric endocrinology, pediatric hematology, etc.).

Since many of the symptoms of anxiety and fear can be brought about by physical causes, it is essential that the child receive a physical exam prior to referral for psychological help. The pediatrician is the person most qualified to conduct this. Once the doctor has examined the child and has found no organic cause for the problem, he or she may take one of several steps.

The child may be referred to a subspecialist for additional medical examinations. For example, for children with severe persistent headaches, a checkup by a neurologist may be in order. In the case of a bedwetter, a urologist may be consulted.

The pediatrician may decide that the problem is psychological and choose to handle it himself. Pediatricians vary in the degree of formal training they receive in psychology, psychiatry, and child development. The experienced pediatrician has examined thousands of children and despite lack of formal training in child development may possess an excellent *experiential* basis for making decisions in this area. Thus, he will know which problems are normal and likely to disappear and which require extended treatment. Pediatricians generally do not take on the prolonged psychological care of a child. A referral to a mental health professional is most common—and recommended—in such cases.

Clinical Psychologist

The clinical psychologist is a specialist in the evaluation and treatment of behavioral and emotional problems. He or she is not medically trained and thus does not prescribe medication or perform surgery. The psychologist's training consists of a doctorate (usually a Ph.D but sometimes a Psy.D. or Ed.D.) in clinical psychology earned at an accredited university or professional school plus a minimum of two years of clinical training, one of which must be post-doctoral. Like the physician, the psychologist must pass a state licensing exam in order to be qualified to practice. Since there are individuals who falsely pass themselves off as psychologists, parents who are unsure of the qualifications of a specific individual should inquire regarding his state *license to practice psychology*. (The qualified professional, be he psychologist or physician, will not resent questions about his qualifications. In fact, if a doctor seems overly defensive or hostile to such questioning, parents should regard this as a danger sign.)

A comprehensive list of many licensed psychologists can be found in the *National Register of Health Service Providers in Psychology*. This book can be found at many libraries, or inquiries can be addressed to: The National Register at 1200 Seventeenth Street, N.W., Washington, D.C., 20036. Information regarding licensure of an individual psychologist can be obtained by contacting the local Board of Medical Examiners.

In deciding upon a clinical psychologist, parents should seek someone who specializes in work with children. The clinical child psychologist, of all health professionals, is most likely to understand child development in depth. He or she is trained to be aware of which behaviors are normal at various age levels and which are unusual. The psychologist is also a specialist in psychological evaluation and testing.

Psychiatrist

The psychiatrist is a physician (M.D. or D.O.) who has received specialty training in the medical treatment of mental disease. Psychiatric training takes place during an internship and two to three years of residency past the Doctorate. The psychiatrist can prescribe drugs and should be consulted in cases where medication is called for, such as psychosis or other forms of severe mental disorder. Some psychiatrists specialize in psychotherapy and prescribe little medication, while others are primarily biologically oriented.

The medical license, like the psychologist's license, is a *generic* certification. In other words, any individual with an M.D. who has served a one-year internship and passed a state board examination is fully licensed to practice *any type of medicine he pleases*. The general practitioner may legally call himself a neurosurgeon, pediatrician, or psychiatrist, although to do so is rare. Aside from the question of ethics, there is the high risk of malpractice suits. Still and all, parents seeking psychiatric help for a seriously disturbed child should inquire about the physician's *board certification* in psychiatry. In addition, there are subspecialty boards in *child psychiatry*. While subspecialty certification is not an automatic indicator of competence, the parent will know that the psychiatrist has received extensive training in the medical treatment of children with mental disorders.

In cases where long-term prescription of psychotropic medication (drugs that affect psychological processes, such as tranquilizers and stimulants) is indicated, the psychiatrist is best qualified to monitor the child's progress. While most pediatricians feel comfortable prescribing these drugs for short periods of time, they usually do not undertake long-term care of a seriously disturbed child without psychiatric or psychological consultation.

While psychologists and psychiatrists share some professional functions—counseling, psychotherapy, mental health consultation—each profession has its area of expertise and specialization. The psychologist has extensive training in normal behavior and child development, as well as in psychological evaluation, while the psychiatrist's medical training makes his or her input essential in cases where pharmacologic management of serious mental disorders, such as psychosis, is indicated.

There are certain qualities that parents should look for in any therapist.

A Readiness to Answer Inquiries about Qualification. As has been mentioned, the qualified doctor will not resent polite inquiries regarding his or her training. Improper psychological or psychiatric care is not only ineffective; it can exacerbate problems. In addition, it is expensive. Parents should think of themselves as consumers of a service—health care—and should make every effort to obtain the best help possible.

Rapport. A doctor may be highly qualified, and yet the parent or child may not feel comfortable with him. Rapport can build gradually, while the child takes his time in bestowing trust in an outsider. But there will be relationships that show no promise of developing rapport. Effective psychological care depends upon a positive, trusting relationship between therapist and patient; feelings of resentment or distrust can hamper treatment. Sometimes doctors and patients mesh and sometimes they don't.

Parents should not remain with a psychotherapist who does not inspire trust and positive feelings. In all but the smallest towns there will be many mental health professionals from whom to choose. Of course, parents who find themselves "doctor hopping"—rushing from therapist to therapist without finding someone with whom they feel comfortable—might examine whether the problem is personal reluctance to enter a psychotherapeutic situation.

Explanation of Treatment Goals and Procedures. Health services occupy a broad range in terms of how clearly they can be defined. There is little ambiguity concerning the process of surgery or its goals: an attempt is made to repair a defect mechanically or to remove troublesome tissue. The practice of nonsurgical medicine is somewhat less precise. Medications, exercises, and dietary routines are prescribed with much less certainty as to their outcome. However, in medicine precise calibration of dosage can often be determined.

On the extremely ambiguous end of the spectrum are mental health services. Some people regard the practice of psychotherapy as a lot of hocus-pocus—some of this feeling is justified. Partial blame must rest with psychotherapists who have devised elaborate but ill-defined treatment techniques without scientific evidence to verify them. Nevertheless, there has been strong progress in defining emotional problems and treatments during the past fifty years. Psychologists have explored behavioral approaches, while psychiatrists, psychologists, and pharmacologists have investigated the biological processes behind emotions and behavior. The consumer of mental health services has the right to ask for and receive *specific information* about what is going to be done during treatment.

The psychotherapist should be able to explain *clearly* his assessment of the problem, once an evaluation has been completed. He should be expected to define the type of treatment recommended and the goals. Parents should shy away from doctors who offer them jargon-laden answers or otherwise cloud their explanations so that they don't make sense. In my own practice, I try to see to it that the child and his parents know as much about what is going on in treatment as I do. Since the success of therapy depends so much upon the youngster's and parent's active participation, I view patient education as essential. This is also in accord with the main concept of this book: Children who understand what is happening to them develop greater mastery and control over their feelings and behavior.

Of course there may be times when the therapist and child

need to discuss personal issues in an atmosphere of *confidentiality*. The doctor may not wish to divulge specific information to parents; however, parents should expect to receive at least general input regarding the treatment plan.

Emphasis upon Minimal Treatment. Children are much more resilient and flexible than are adults. Because of this they respond successfully to brief psychological treatment. Some children with severe emotional problems will require a long-term psychotherapy. Even so, children should be offered the least amount of treatment that is effective and no more. The ethical psychotherapist will not attempt to keep a basically normal child in treatment for prolonged periods of time.

While the psychologist or psychiatrist may not be able to predict exactly how long treatment will last, doctors should provide a *general* response along these lines. Ask whether the therapist's orientation is toward long-term or short-term treatment (my own particular bias for the latter is clearly obvious) and if the answer is long-term, make sure that the severity of the child's problem justifies this.

Treatment Settings

Pediatricians, clinical psychologists, and child psychiatrists generally practice privately, on a fee-for-service basis. Pediatricians charge for procedures—a certain fee is assigned to a checkup, another to an injection, etc. Psychologists and psychiatrists usually charge for their time. The therapeutic "hour" is either forty-five or fifty minutes and the range of fees is approximately thirty-five to one hundred dollars per "hour."

Many insurance plans will reimburse policy holders for a portion of the psychotherapeutic charge. When economic factors prevent parents from seeking help in a private setting, they should inquire about child guidance clinics, which are funded

partially through private fees as well as a variety of public funds. Services are usually offered on a "sliding scale"—the fee is based upon the family's ability to pay. Some clinics and community mental health centers offer free psychological care. The child may see a psychologist or psychiatrist at a guidance clinic, or he may be treated by a psychology intern, psychiatric resident, or other mental health trainee—under the supervision of a licensed doctor.

Mental health services are also offered at many university psychology departments or in the psychiatry divisions of local hospitals. Here, too, the child is likely to be seen by someone in training who is being supervised by a fully licensed psychologist or psychiatrist. Sometimes the best treatment available is through a university or medical school, because these are the centers where contemporary mental health research is conducted, and doctors with academic affiliations are aware of the most up-to-date treatment approaches.

Parents should not assume that the axiom "You get what you pay for" applies to psychotherapists on an individual basis. I am aware of doctors who charge exorbitant fees—substantially above the local average—but whose skills are less than average. Conversely, there are many fine therapists who choose to maintain a moderate fee system. Fees are often set in accordance with geographical rather than competence criteria—doctors in high-rent areas may charge more. Given the wide variety of mental health settings available, there is no reason why economic factors should prevent a troubled child from receiving psychological help.

Treatment Approaches

Psychotherapists differ in terms of theoretical and practical training. In contrast with medicine, where procedures are

roughly (but not totally) equivalent, psychotherapists employ a wide variety of techniques and philosophies, including the following:

Psychoanalysis. The goal in Freudian psychoanalysis is to uncover deep-seated, "subconscious" conflicts that are thought to be the cause of problematic behaviors. According to orthodox analytic theory, sexuality is the major area of conflict. The psychoanalyst interprets anxious or fearful behavior as symptomatic of an underlying conflict rather than as a problem in itself. He or she does not attempt to treat the fearful reaction. directly. Psychoanalysis with children usually takes the form of play therapy as well as talking. Traditional psychoanalysis is a lengthy process, during which the patient sees the analyst several times a week. Less orthodox analytic approaches make use of short-term treatment and have deemphasized sexuality. Analysts who follow the teachings of Jung, Adler, or others differ in their theoretical orientation, particularly concerning the importance of sexuality. However, they, too, consider anxiety and fear as symptoms, not problems.

I consider psychoanalysis a fine way for a generally well-adjusted adult to learn about himself. Children also may profit from some of the tangential aspects of analysis—the warmth and support offered by the analyst, the encouragement of emotional expression. However there is no substantial scientific evidence supporting the usefulness of psychoanalysis in curing children's anxiety reactions.

Behavior Therapy. This approach, the one emphasized in this book, grew out of experimental psychology. Behavior therapy is a specific application of behavior modification (a much used, somewhat vulgarized term that describes the application of learning principles in a variety of settings—clinic, school, advertising, etc.), and it is practiced by a qualified psychologist or physician. Behavior therapists view psychological problems as learned behaviors that have gained strength due to modeling, association, payoff, or any combination of these.

Behavior therapy usually involves short-term treatment and is highly effective in the amelioration of problematic fear and anxiety. It does not bring about total cure in seriously disturbed individuals, such as psychotics, although it can be used to improve the behavior of psychotic patients (by encouraging self-help skills, reducing bizarre speech, etc).

Early critics of behavior therapy claimed that rapid removal of symptoms did not represent a true cure, because the underlying conflict had not been dealt with. According to this theory, a new symptom was sure to appear, taking the place of the old one. However, such *symptom substitution* did not occur, when the matter was researched. The effectiveness of behavior therapy makes it a definite treatment of choice for many types of anxiety-related disorders.

Some have also claimed that the techniques of behavior therapy are too mechanical. However insensitive treatment is not the province of any one form of therapy but a matter of the sensitivity of the therapist.

Family Therapy. This is a specific *method* of therapy involving treatment of the family unit, as opposed to the individual patient. Family therapy is conducted by therapists with a wide range of theoretical orientations. Some family therapists apply psychoanalytic principles—gaining insight about subconscious conflicts that exist in the entire family. Many behavior therapists work with families in changing patterns of learned behavior. In fact, most psychologists and psychiatrists who work primarily with children spend a good deal of time with parents. To the extent that problems are seen as resulting from family interactions, these doctors will frequently see child and parents at the same time. One major form of family therapy is practiced by Dr. Salvador Minuchin and others, whereby an attempt is made to alter family *patterns of communication*. According to this school of thought, psychological problems are the result of contradictory or confused interpersonal messages. Dr. Minuchin's creative techniques have been successfully used for anorexia nervosa and other problems.

Family therapy is based on a fact of life: Behavior is heavily influenced by the *environment*. Family therapy emphasizes the interaction between a person and his family environment, demonstrating differences in the way people react to one member of the family or another. It is clearly an important therapeutic technique with which the qualified psychologist or psychiatrist should be familiar.

Play Therapy. Like family therapy, play therapy is a modality, not a school of thought. Since children, especially young children, often express themselves in nonverbal ways, it makes sense to communicate with them through drawing and playing. Child psychoanalysts will attempt to get at subconscious conflicts through the use of play. Hospital patient activity specialists will prepare young patients for medical procedures using play. Behavior therapists teach children to learn counter-anxious behaviors, such as anger by utilizing a play therapy approach. For this reason, play therapy must be considered a *vehicle* for change rather than a panacean solution to children's emotional problems. It makes no more sense for a psychotherapist to say "I use only play therapy" or "I'm a play therapist" than it does for a surgeon to boast "I do all my operations with only one scalpel."

In addition to its usefulness as a therapeutic tool, play therapy is a good way of building rapport with the young patient. Because play is relaxing and encourages flights of fantasy, it is therapeutically counter-anxious.

Hypnosis. There is no psychological technique more fraught with mystery, misconception, and fear than hypnosis.

Media representations of hypnosis have caused many children and adults to believe that it involves being under the control of another person, that hypnotized people are silly, and that the capacity to be hypnotized (susceptibility) connotes weakness and stupidity. None of these beliefs is true.

All forms of *hypnosis are, in fact, self-hypnosis.* The phenomenon, hard to define, occurs when an individual combines relaxation with focused concentration and becomes more suggestible—open to new ideas. In the absence of drugs, hypnosis is a *voluntary* process—people can come in and out of a hypnotic state at will—and it is heavily influenced by a person's belief system. Far from representing loss of control, hypnosis is a form of *enhanced self-control.* Under hypnosis, many people are able to experience reduced pain, improved memory, and distortions of time (shortening *or* lengthening of time perception). Some individuals can undergo memory loss (amnesia) for selected events. And hypnotic susceptibility is related to *greater,* not lesser intelligence, probably because it depends upon imagination, creativity, and the ability to concentrate.

No one knows why hypnosis works. There have been biochemical, neurological, psychological, and sociological explanations offered for the very real phenomena that occur during hypnosis. Many of these theories appear promising. However the process of hypnosis remains poorly understood. The clinical usefulness of hypnosis has been known for centuries—surgeons in sixteenth-century India performed major operations utilizing hypnosis as sole anesthesia. We are thus faced with a treatment technique that works despite the fact that we don't understand why it is effective.

Children between the ages of six and ten make the best hypnotic subjects. Their heightened sense of fantasy and lack of inhibition make it easy for them to focus upon an imaginary theme, as compared to adults and teen-agers, who tend to be somewhat skeptical. In addition, children of primary school age have sufficient concentration to enter the hypnotic state; youngsters of three and four may have difficulty with this. Most children over four are somewhat hypnotizable. For this reason hypnosis is an excellent pediatric technique *in the hands of a trained psychologist, physician or dentist.*

Hypnosis is not a cure-all. It is one of several techniques the qualified therapist should have at his disposal. This excludes so-called *lay hypnotists*—individuals who do not possess training in health care but who have learned how to induce hypnosis. (Since hypnosis is a natural process, the ability to hypnotize can be taught to almost anyone with normal intelligence.) Though many states recognize the legal right of lay hypnotists to practice, I regard them as untrained in the treatment of emotional disorders, especially with regard to children. Lay hypnotists are likely to see hypnosis as a panacea. They are likely to make outrageous and unrealistic claims and to create false hope. Even more serious, the lay hypnotist, untrained at recognizing when *not* to use hypnosis, may induce a hypnotic state in a seriously disturbed individual in whom excessive fantasy is dangerous. Since there are many qualified doctors who are trained in hypnosis, there is no reason for parents to bring their child to an untrained hypnotist for hypnotherapy.

One additional note regarding the relationship between hypnosis and suggestion: *Hypnoidal* or hypnotic-like states occur almost every day in children of normal intelligence. The youngster who watches a movie and feels himself part of the story is undergoing a hypnoidal experience. Similarly, the child who becomes so engrossed in a book that he loses track of time or doesn't hear someone calling him is in a hypnotic-like state: The combination of relaxation and focused attention has shut him off from outside distractions. It is not that the sounds of traffic or blaring music have disappeared. The child's mind has simply blocked them out. This is an especially useful concept when applied to pain. At Childrens Hospital of Los Angeles, my colleagues and I have conducted research that shows hypnosis to be effective in reducing pain and nausea in some children with cancer. Other researchers have produced encouraging results in ameliorating pain due to burns, dental work, and surgery. Hypnosis is clearly a valuable tool that needs to be investigated further.

Because *hypnotic-like states are normal,* the child need not be under hypnosis in order to respond to suggestion. Parents can use suggestion in helping children to overcome anxiety and fear. A reassuring hand upon the shoulder combined with a "you-can-handle it" message goes a long way in establishing positive expectations.

Hypnosis has been used successfully in treating bedwetting, soiling, and other problems. It may be used by itself or combined with approaches that suggest relaxation, comfort, and self-control.

16

The Limits of Protection

Being a parent means assuming many different roles. A parent is a provider of nourishment and basic material comfort, giver of love and emotional support, teacher, guide, model, and *protector*. Because it is our responsibility to shield our children from danger, we are likely to feel extremely guilty if harm befalls them. "Where did I go wrong?" is a question many parents ask, even though we may not have been able to prevent the danger. Our guilt comes about almost reflexively as we accept the Protector Role.

We cannot always be there to protect our children. Falls, scrapes, and minor accidents of childhood are inevitable and impossible to prevent. We cannot protect youngsters indefinitely, and if we hover over them we keep them from developing normal patterns of adaptation. Of course, it is important to take reasonable safety precautions and to create a home environment where accidents are unlikely to occur. However, it is unwise to bring a child up in an atmosphere of constant fearfulness, teaching him by example that the world is a dangerous and threatening place. Much of what happens to children—and adults—depends upon *chance* (Providence, Fate, or whatever one calls it). Brian, the boy with the fear of Dracula, simply happened to watch a specific movie while he was in a period of particular vulnerability. His subsequent problems were unique and impossible to predict, making prevention highly unlikely. And so it is with many children who experience threatening and frightening stimuli, accidentally or otherwise.

Today's parents find it difficult to shield children from disturbing information. The mass media—especially television and motion pictures—increasingly influence the attitudes and behavior of children. There is little research concerning the effects of motion pictures and television on children's anxiety. We certainly know of numerous instances where viewing a particular program or film has had an extremely adverse effect. However, we lack scientific studies as to which children are particularly vulnerable, what types of programs are especially anxiety provoking, and other issues.

The relationship between media viewing and *aggression* has been researched, and there is a substantial body of knowledge to indicate that youngsters who watch violence on the screen are more likely to exhibit overly aggressive behavior than those who do not. A strong case can be made for reducing childrens' access to television *apart* from any connection between viewing and anxiety.

The average American child spends more time watching television than engaging in any other single activity except sleeping. Some simple calculations will illustrate the pervasiveness of TV. Consider the youngster who begins viewing at age three and continues through the age of seventeen. During this fourteen-year period, if he watches TV for 20 hours per week, his total viewing time will be 14,560 hours

(20 × 52 × 14). When we realize that 20 hours is a conservative figure for many children (The youngster who watches three hours a day during the week and five hours each on Saturday and Sunday, will compile a 25-hour weekly total), the *quantitative* impact of TV is staggering. Let us examine some research findings into the influence of this powerful medium.

There is strong evidence that television serves as a means of *preventing communication* between family members. A study done in Iceland, comparing families with high access to television to those with limited access, found a high rate of viewing to be associated with poor psychological adjustment in children. This may have been because youngsters with tendencies to psychological difficulties gravitate most strongly to TV or to the fact that children who are prevented from developing interpersonal skills because they are constantly glued to the screen never learn how to deal effectively with emotional issues.

Commentary on both the role of the American father and the effect of TV upon the family is present in a study conducted by Dr. J. R. Jung, of Longwood College. One hundred and fifty-six preschoolers were questioned about their attitudes about television, and *44 percent replied that they preferred TV to Daddy*. When one considers that children are likely to model the behavior of those whom they admire, questions arise as to who *really* influences the twentieth-century child.

Research at the University of Minnesota has indicated that families who watched a great deal of TV tended to exhibit a high degree of interpersonal tension between parents and teenagers. The Minnesota researchers posit that many families may use TV as a means of escaping conflict. Notable among these findings is the fact that the content of the shows watched was not considered—what is being emphasized is the escapist nature of the medium itself.

Recent brain-wave research indicates that children who

watch television are likely to enter into a state of consciousness similar to presleep relaxation. In other words, the popular notion of TV as a form of *hypnosis* appears scientifically valid. It is important to understand that hypnosis is neither bad nor good—it is a neutral state during which the individual is increasingly susceptible to new information. Let us examine the *quality* of information that youngsters receive while entering the video-hypnotic state.

Television presents a host of models from which children can learn, many of them unsavory. In their book *The Youth Market: Its Dimensions, Influence and Opportunities for You,* Melvin Helitzer and Carl Heyel advise television sponsors how to pick "the right character for your product."

". . . if you want to create your own hard-hitting spokesman to children, the most effective route is the superhero—miracle worker. He certainly can demonstrate food products, drug items, many kinds of toys and innumerable items."

How do these experts describe the ideal superhero?

"The character should be adventurous. And he should be on the right side of the law. A child must be able to mimic his hero, whether he is James Bond, Superman, or Dick Tracy; to be able to fight and shoot to kill without punishment or guilt feelings."

A casual inspection of typical TV fare shows that this sage advice has been followed closely by the television networks. Parents need seriously to consider whether shooting to kill (in the name of what's right, of course) without guilt is the type of behavior they wish their children to model.

TV shows give a distorted view of the world. Apart from an excessive preoccupation with violence, television creates unnatural expectations on the part of children—and adults. On TV, even the most serious problems are solved by the third commercial, and often the "cure" is effected in a simplistic and unrealistic manner.

Dr. Christina Nystrom of New York University has suggested that television compresses life into an exceptionally narrow context and leads children to overemphasize immediate gratification. As such, she feels, TV has contributed to a decline in rational thought, analysis, reflection, and patience.

I feel that some instances of the so-called "hyperactivity" syndrome, a major symptom of which is shortened attention span, may be associated with heavy TV viewing. During the quasi-hypnotic state that takes place during TV viewing children are unable to focus or attend to specific program content but react to the *emotional arousal* of the medium. Brain-wave tracings indicate that most youngsters are unable to sustain attention for more than a fraction of a half-hour viewing period. This is not the case in other learning activities, such as reading. Thus, children who constantly watch TV may be progressively *learning not to pay attention*. Even educational television has been implicated in this regard. Many teachers observe that children who have been brought up on a steady diet of shows where information is constantly offered in a rapid, noisy, highly stimulating manner, have difficulties sitting still in class and engaging in quieter forms of learning.

An additional disturbing note regarding television comes from a study at Michigan State University which found that emotionally disturbed children most strongly identified with stereotypic information presented on the screen. Thus, those youngsters who are most likely to be adversely affected by what they see on the screen appear to be those who really take television seriously.

In addition, the information presented to children on TV may be highly inaccurate and potentially damaging. I recently viewed a popular situation comedy in which an adult character explained the death of a loved one to a child. The essence of the explanation went something like this:

"Well, Bobby, you know how you and I get tired and have to go to sleep? That's what happened to Grandpa—he got very tired and is going to rest for a long, long time."

The child accepted this explanation cheerfully and the explainer then turned to another adult and said:

"See? Isn't that simple."

This was followed by a tumultous wave of canned laughter.

No comment.

In summary, we see that television is potentially destructive in several ways: First, *no matter what is on the screen,* the video medium itself induces a hypnotic-like state that may cause short attention span. The pervasive nature of TV allows it to block out interpersonal communication and provides an escape for those who wish to avoid dealing with emotional issues. Extensive television viewing takes the place of more active, constructive activities on both individual and family levels, and breeds passivity. In addition, the content of many television shows is overly violent, often inaccurate, and models attitudes and behaviors that are not conducive to intellectual and psychological growth.

Frightening information protrayed on TV and in the movies has greater potential to traumatize youngsters than does the same information transmitted through the written word. When a child watches something violent on the screen, he is powerless to stop it. A film goes on at a predetermined pace, leaving the child no control other than to leave the room. Reading, however, requires *active* participation. The child is able to stop and go as he pleases and has the ability to achieve mastery over potentially frightening material. There are few instances of children who are traumatized by books, but many youngsters become severely frightened by violent movies and TV shows.

Some people feel that the government should monitor the

quality of childrens' television. I do not feel that the answer lies in more "big-brotherly" supervision. First of all, the nature of what is being shown is only part of the problem. No matter how "constructive" TV shows become, there will always be a psychological danger in extensive TV viewing *per se*. And more important, it is essential that parents exercise their rights and decide that they, not an impersonal agency, shall guide their children.

Take control of the set and expect repercussions. Children who are accustomed to watching television for three hours a day will protest vigorously when their viewing time is reduced. In fact, they may exhibit withdrawal symptoms as their addiction is curtailed. Parents must offer specific alternatives to watching TV—it is not enough to tell the child what he cannot do. He needs constructive replacement behaviors. Furthermore, parents cannot expect to continue their own habitual viewing while demanding abstinence from the child. The challenge is to cut the video umbilical cord for all members of the family. Parents and children should learn how to talk to each other and how to participate actively in cooperative, pleasurable activities.

Having constructed a rather strong case against heavy television viewing, the following statement may seem paradoxical:

Children who have been frightened by something on TV or film should not be restricted from viewing that same show, or something similar to it. Parents should take reasonable precautions to screen shows their young children see, but once the child has seen something frightening, he should be allowed to view it repeatedly if he so chooses—in order to learn how to master his fear. I would not advise taking a seven-year-old to see *Jaws* in the first place. However, the youngster who has been traumatized by *Jaws* may profit from viewing the shark several times, until it no longer elicits anxiety, if he so wishes.

Parents should not make a big fuss about keeping children from specific films because they are too frightening. A suggestion of one or more alternative films is helpful, for example, "I don't feel this movie would be the best for you, but how about. . . ." The reasons for not allowing a child to see a specific show should not be *personalized*—the child should not be told "You cannot see this film because you can't handle it." A more general approach should be adopted, such as "I don't think this show is good for any kid of eight."

It is also important to understand that what an adult considers frightening may not arouse anxiety in a child. A preschool youngster may be less concerned about a murder than with the fact that a child portrayed on the screen is being abandoned by his parents. Similarly, a child of nine or ten may concentrate upon what he perceives as physically painful events, though these may be tangential to the plot. Parents should familiarize themselves with the show or film they are prohibiting, but should avoid hasty, restrictive decisions. Too much prohibition of a child's viewing material can lead him to think that his parents expect him to become afraid. When a doubt arises regarding the appropriateness of a specific film or show, it is often best to allow the child to view it, perhaps in the presence of familiar people, when anxiety is likely to be lower.

Parents should also be prepared to answer the child's questions about emotionally laden material. Television shows and motion pictures that cause family members to communicate with each other can play a constructive role. While TV group-viewing cannot be considered a family activity—it is merely a collection of people, each immersed in a semi-hypnotic state—discussions of what has been viewed can open up channels of expression. (Unfortunately, much of what is portrayed on the screen is not exceptionally thought-provoking.)

Television, of course, has great potential as a therapeutic

and educational tool. Videotapes have been used to help prepare patients for surgery and other medical experiences. Self-paced, computerized teaching packages can be effectively presented in video form. However, in order to have optimum benefit, TV must allow the viewer control over the pace and content of broadcast. The child or adult should be able to take charge and "talk back" to the television. In this regard, commercial television is unlikely to change from what it is now—a highly effective electronic babysitter that spoon-feeds entertainment to passive recipients. It can relax, soothe, and arouse viewers, and it can sell products. But it will seldom enrich its audience.

SELECTED READINGS

Azrin, Nathan and Foxx, Richard, M. *Toilet Training in Less Than a Day*. New York: Simon and Schuster, 1974. Drs. Azrin and Foxx describe, in detail, techniques to help teach children *who are physically ready* to develop appropriate toilet behaviors. The emphasis is upon rewarding desired behaviors and minimizing punishment and needless anxiety. Much of this material grew out of Azrin and Foxx's work with severely retarded youngsters and generalizes, with ease, to healthy children.

Benson, Herbert. *The Relaxation Response*. Boston: G. K. Hall, 1976. Dr. Benson is a prominent authority in the field of behavioral medicine at Harvard Medical School. His background of extensive research and clinical experience is well utilized in this book, which describes theoretical and practical aspects of human relaxation. An excellent layman's guide for adults who are interested in knowing more about how anxiety affects the body as well as how to gain greater control over stress.

Grollman, Earl A. *Explaining Death to Children*. Boston: Beacon Press, 1967. In this edited volume, still considered a classic, Dr. Grollman has assembled a wide range of psychological, religious, anthropological, and philosophical essays concerning children and death. Erudite, but concisely written, these articles are comprehensive and informative. Of particular interest to parents are chapters on talking to children of different ages about death and a reference section on books for children that deal with death, dying and related topics.

Patterson, Gerald R. *Families*. Champaign, Ill.: Research Press, 1971. A readable volume demonstrating how principles of learning can be applied to everyday child-rearing situations. Dr. Patterson's emphasis is on normal issues that arise in normal families. He is a professor of psychology at the University of Oregon and his books grow out of extensive research conducted at the Social Learning Project in Eugene, Ore.

Salk, Lee. *What Every Child Would Like His Parents to Know About Divorce*. New York: Harper & Row, 1978. Divorce is a growing source of stress for adults and children. If properly handled —through psychological preparation—it needn't bring about major disruption for most youngsters. Dr. Salk, a well-known pediatric psychologist, wrote this book after the breakup of his own marriage. Like most of his books, it is clear, compassionate, and has a personal flavor. Dr. Salk discusses how to communicate the facts and feelings of divorce to children in order to minimize psychological side-effects.

INDEX